The Forgiveness of Sins

The Forgiveness of Sins

AN ESSAY IN THE HISTORY OF
CHRISTIAN DOCTRINE AND PRACTICE

by

W. TELFER, D.D.
Fellow of Selwyn College, Cambridge

SCM PRESS LTD
56 BLOOMSBURY STREET
LONDON

FIRST PUBLISHED 1959
© SCM PRESS LTD 1959
PRINTED IN GREAT BRITAIN BY
THE BOWERING PRESS
PLYMOUTH

Contents

THIS book originated in lectures given at a conference of the Student Christian Movement and subsequently revised for three diocesan Clergy Schools. I owe grateful thanks to those who helped me by their contributions to the discussions after the lectures, and to those who asked that they should be printed.

W.T.

Prologue

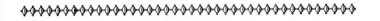

ANYONE who chanced upon this little book might wonder why there should be need, at this date, to write about the forgiveness of sins. Is not the Christian doctrine on this subject fully and clearly set forth in Scripture, and above all in the New Testament? No doubt the answer to this question must be in the affirmative. But that would not be a complete answer, for if the modern Christian reader should be unconsciously reading his own ideas on this subject into scriptural language by which the authors meant something different, this would amount to a misreading of Scripture. It will form part of the argument of this book that this is what very commonly happens. For example, we read, in many places, of God's free forgiveness of those who repent and believe. But to whom were these passages addressed? We cannot safely apply them now without taking that into account. Are they to be taken as promises of a once-for-all forgiveness attached to conversion? Or is it clear that they were so intended as to apply to Christians when they repent of having fallen away from their baptismal purity? Should it be that we are, for any reason, disposed to think too lightly of forgiveness, we may very easily put upon the words of Scripture a meaning which the writers did not intend. For example, let us suppose that an open-minded and careful study of the language of the New Testament in its context brought us to the conclusion that the first Christians had no idea, after their entry by baptism into a new covenant with God, of ever again committing offences against him. It would then be incredible that writers of the first Christian age would mean to suggest that baptized Christians would commit and repent new sins repeatedly: although that is something which the modern Christian habitually assumes. And if there is, here, a possibility of our misinterpreting the New Testament, there is room for re-examination of the whole question.

On the other hand, it might be asked whether any historical approach to the subject of the forgiveness of sins is needed. Could not a philosopher of religion, it might be asked, set out, once for all, a sufficient doctrine of the forgiveness of sins, based simply upon the attributes of God, and the nature of man and of sin? That road certainly cannot be declared 'no thoroughfare' until it has been tried.

Our philosopher would have to start with the notions of sin and forgiveness which obtain in the field of human social relations. In that field, the natural reaction of a person sinned against is to retaliate. In life lived at an animal level, retaliation for offence is automatic and inevitable. But human culture gives rise to considerations which restrain or modify such reaction. The desire for retaliation may depart altogether, if the offender shows that his offence was not intentional; for it is at least as much the intention as the behaviour that constitutes the sin, where civilized men and women are concerned. Even where the sin was, at the time, deliberate, the same result may follow, if the offender, afterwards, comes to a different mind and shows sincere concern to make amends. As the sin took place in time past, he cannot undo it. But he can so desire to dissociate himself from his sin as to prevail upon the offended person to restore their mutual relations to cordiality. Yielding to this generous impulse, he will think no more of retaliation. And it is this act of generosity that bears the name of forgiveness.

The English word 'forgive' (like French *pardonner* and German *vergeben*) is simply a strengthened form of the verb to give or grant. And the reason for adopting this strengthened word-form is to emphasize the unconditional nature of the act which it represents. Now if the waiving of retaliation is to be unconditional, it must spring from kindness and good will on the part of the person who forgives. For if a person were to renounce retaliation because he feared the offender, or because he hoped, by so doing, to gain some future benefit by means of him, it would be no sign of kindness or good will. Furthermore, such renunciation would not be unconditional, and so could not rightly be called forgiveness.

The possibility of forgiveness also depends upon the state of mind of the offender. If, so far from wishing to dissociate himself from the offence, he would willingly repeat it, the offender opposes an insuperable obstacle to the generosity of the other party, so that, however good and kind they may be, they cannot attain to actual forgiveness of the offender. In that case, the most they can do is to withhold retaliation, so as to oppose no obstacle to a change of heart on the part of the offender, while dismissing the memory of the offence from having any influence upon their own feelings. It would be wrong, however, to confuse just and prudent punishment with retaliation, in such a situation. There is a deep distinction between them. The sting of retaliation lies in the personal feeling of hostility that accompanies it. This creates or increases enmity between the parties, from which both find it difficult to recover. Punishment that is clearly not retaliation does not have this effect, and so does not create an obstacle to reconciliation; so that, if the feeling of the person sinned against continues to be kind and good, a change of mind on the part of the offender can come to fulfilment. Until that change takes place, however, the party sinned against must be content to be 'not overcome of evil'. They cannot 'overcome evil with good' by forgiving. They can, indeed, go on hoping for a change of heart on the part of the offender, and their hope can be called the earnest, or even the substance, of forgiveness; but it is not forgiveness itself, until the offender makes that possible.

At this point we must take notice of the part played by the time factor, in this drama of sin and forgiveness. Passage of time is the reason why the sinner cannot alter what has been done, but can only seek to dissociate himself from it. It is the passage of time, again, that contains the hope of his change of heart. And because both parties are subject to time, the behaviour of the person sinned against must ever wait upon that of the sinner. These are the main facts about the forgiveness, as it takes place in human life. How far do they illuminate divine forgiveness of the sins of men?

In the first place, God cannot be supposed subject to the passage of time, in the way that men are. Consequently, when we would apply ideas of sin and forgiveness derived from human relationships to divine forgiveness of man's sin, we must exclude the notion of human action being followed by divine reaction. We may rightly deduce, from the attributes of God, that he hates sin and loves the sinning creature. But, if so, he must do both things at once and timelessly. On the other hand, if God is, in any real sense, personal, the fundamental or final unwillingness of a sinner to be dissociated from his sin must oppose an insuperable obstacle to forgiveness, no less where the forgiver is God than where he is a good man. This appears to follow logically from the nature of the relations between personal beings. But it is also the unmistakable teaching of the Gospels that a man can so sin as to remove from himself the possibility of being forgiven. The primary text is Mark 3.29, where the main verb is in the future tense, so that the saying takes the form of a warning rather than a pronouncement: 'Whosoever shall blaspheme against the Holy Spirit hath never forgiveness'. (The 'Western' text says 'is guilty of an agelong sin'.) We here see a contrasting of time and eternity. There are sins where, in time, impenitence ends in a change of heart, and there is sinning from which there is never penitence. We cannot suppose that when there is a change of heart on the part of the sinner, this involves any change on God's part, who, from the beginning of creation, foresees that impenitence will end, and has already forgiven from all eternity. We might as well regard a man's repentance as the consequence of divine forgiveness as its cause. But it is possible for man, in his self-determination, to sin decisively what the 'Western' text calls 'an agelong sin'.

The parallel passages in Matthew and Luke (Matt. 12.32; Luke 12.10) give proof that reflection had taken place, upon the episode as recorded in Mark, before their composition. They imply that the Father had given, through his Son, a sign of the Kingdom. And if he gave such a sign, he gave also the power of mind and heart to comprehend it. If, therefore, the Jews misinterpreted the sign, so as to name it a 'devil's wonder', it was because, deep down in their souls, they had encountered the divine Spirit, face to face, and, in their self-pride, had blasphemed him. This was no offence by blunder or mistake, to be rectified upon a later recognition of the truth. Nor was it the impulsive contumacy that is presently followed by a reaction of shame and sorrow. The sin against the Holy Ghost is a determined impenitence whereby a moral creature severs himself fatally from the life of the one true and living God.

There is a further commentary upon the 'agelong sin' in two

passages in Acts (5.1–10; 8.9–24). One tells the dreadful fate of Ananias and Sapphira. The other records the dubious case of Simon Magus; and this passage ends, like our Gospel passage in Mark, on a note of stern warning. It is true that Christian tradition implies that the warning was not regarded. Perhaps the unworthy thought in Simon's heart which St Peter rebuked was but the sign of an inward self-worship by which Simon severed himself from God. But the word of Scripture stops short of any such conclusion, and so leaves us to reflect that however desperate a sin may seem to us to be, it is always possible, while earthly life is granted to the sinner, that by some turn of events there will be discovered a willingness on his part to believe in God, and to love him. Until this moment, the possibility may have lain hid even from the man himself. If this happens, it is proof that, whatever blasphemy the man was guilty of, there was not involved that blasphemy against the divine Spirit in the depth of the heart which cancels for ever the possibility of forgiveness. Christians must not, therefore, presume the damnation of any. On the other hand, the common opinion that if God is good he will forgive us, although we neglect to repent, is to be associated with the common holding of a debased conception of man's moral stature and responsibility.

If, then, we must say that a man who does not desire forgiveness cannot be forgiven, can we assume the converse and say that, as soon as a sinner desires God's forgiveness, he can know that he enjoys it? Alas! no; because of the lack of simplicity in the human heart. A man's feeling towards another man is generally simple enough. He is either in a mind to sin against him, or he is in a mind not to sin against him. But when the sinning is not against another man, but against God, the case is different. A sentiment of desire for God's forgiveness can be secretly mingled with some desire to sin, or with doubt of divine goodness. In that event, the sinner, in spite of his fancy that he is penitent, is still at enmity with God, and unwilling to be dissociated from his sin. Such a sentiment is plainly deceptive, and so gives no ground for assurance of forgiveness. 'The heart is deceitful above all things, and it is desperately sick', says Jeremiah (17.9) 'Who can know it?' And how, then, can we accept the expression of any man's feelings as sure criterion of his relations with his Creator? St Paul declares (I Cor. 4.4) 'I know nothing against my-self; yet am I not hereby justified', and his words should serve to warn more mediocre Christians not to presume themselves for-given because they think themselves sincere in their repentance and faith. And if that be so, we must conclude that the philoso-phic road to assurance of forgiveness is a 'no-thoroughfare'.

Even if there were a stronger argument, on these lines, than has here been made out, it can truly be asserted that, in the Christian Church, the ground for hope of forgiveness has never been of a philosophic nature. That hope was first preached as good news, guaranteed by God's action in history. The Christian doctrine of forgiveness was first expounded in relation to the circumstances in which the believers found themselves. And as the circumstances of Christian life have changed, in following ages, so have the terms changed in which Christian teachers have expressed their apprehension of divine forgiveness. And so the main task of this book will be to tell, in brief outline, what Christian men down the centuries have thought and taught about God's forgiveness of human sin, and how men can be assured that they are forgiven. That task must be commenced by making a short examination of the teaching on this subject contained in the canonical Scriptures.

CHAPTER ONE

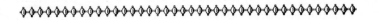

The Biblical Doctrine of Forgiveness

RELIGION creates a sense of personal relation with deity. In the pagan religions which surrounded, first Israel, and then the Christian Church, there was hope of the favour of the gods and fear of offending them, but no thought of their forgiving offences. Forgiveness appeared to be a change of mind, and it would seem beneath the dignity of deity to undergo a change of mind towards mortals. In the God of the Greek philosophers, on the other hand, such an idea as divine forgiveness would be unthinkable, since immutability appeared to be a necessary attribute of deity. The Scriptures of Israel contain signs that Israelite religion, starting from a near-pagan attitude towards offended deity, moved first to a conviction of the partiality of Jehovah towards the children of Israel, and thence to a conception of personal alliance established between Jehovah and Israel. This alliance was explicit in a covenant with undertakings on both sides. Together with this development of theological conception went a growth in ethical sense, on the part of the people. And this sense expressed itself, in turn, in the Israelite conception of the character of the one true and living God. In course of time, this led to a recognition of the contrast between the moral grandeur of God and the moral insufficiency of Israel. So was felt the need of the people for forgiveness, in view of their transgressions of the covenant, recognized not as mischances but

15

as sins. It is this moral perception that makes the religion of Israel so different from, and so superior in religious feeling and theological significance to, the highest expressions of pagan religious thought.

As to the manner of Jehovah's forgiveness of his people, thought began on simple anthropomorphic lines. The righteous God, it was imagined, felt outraged by the sins of his people, but, because of his tenderness towards them, was ready, when they turned away from those sins to do again what was lawful and right, not to impute to them, any more, their former sins. This crudely anthropomorphic way of thinking presently came to be modified as the eternity, might and goodness of God were realized. It is the glory of Ps. 103 to see that God does not react to offences like a man, but shows not only his partiality but his power, in forgiving. Not only does he not impute to us our sins (a thing conceivable on the part of a good man) but he can sever our sins from us, 'as far as the east is from the west'. Such power on the part of God to annihilate the guilt of sins comes to expression again in Micah 7.19, where God is pictured as casting Israel's sins into the depths of the sea.

This assurance of divine forgiveness, on the part of Old Testament saints to whom the Christian Gospel was unknown, poses the question whether, after all, assurance of forgiveness can be had without the Gospel. The explanation of the assurance thus expressed by psalmist and prophet, which accords best with the Old Testament itself, is that they received it by a word of the Lord. This is also an explanation that raises no difficulty for Christian doctrine, which acknowledges that God ever was what now, in Christ, he is manifested to be. For already at the start of the second Christian century, Ignatius of Antioch declared that we see, in the Scriptures of the Old Testament, lights reflected back from the Gospel that was to follow after (*To the Magnesians* cc. 8 and 9). And it is in this sense, of a light reflected back from the cross of Christ, that Ignatius would have regarded the Old Testament belief in the efficacy of sacrifices for sins. It is therefore in this sense of lights reflected back from the Gospel that we may view the hopes, and even the assurance, of forgiveness, that meet us in the pages of the Old Testament.

But this realization of the relation between man the sinner and God the forgiver, so far from diminishing the concern of Israelites for having sinned, deepened and increased it. Accordingly, as we pass to the period between the Testaments, it is to see, in the saints of Israel, a tragic sense of guilt, which accepts adversity as righteous retribution. Yet joined with this was a yearning hope for some final act of God, springing from his power and righteousness, which would not only show and implement his forgiveness of his people, but would crown his rational purpose regarding them, by delivering them from sinfulness. The working of this divine purpose towards Israel was seen as stretching through history, and as now moving towards its end. Forgiveness of Israel's sins was thus seen, not as an incidental, but as an eschatological act of God. Apocalyptic writers of the age between the Testaments strove to pierce the mystery of God's purposes, so as to visualize their happy and triumphal fulfilment. And as the Gospels picture for us the outlook of that generation of Israel into which Christ was born, it is the outlook of a people whose eyes are strained towards such a *dénouement*. It was to this expectancy that John the Baptist addressed himself, declaring its fulfilment to be at hand. He announced that they would shortly see an event, fearful to many, by reason of God's wrath towards the unrepentant, but, to those who sought his face in sincerity, most joyful. The Gospels pass from this prophesying of John to des-

B

cribe the ministry of Christ as in full continuity with it. Nevertheless, between John's preaching and the preaching of Jesus, there is a marked change of tone. Jesus set faith in the good purposes of the heavenly Father before preoccupation with the sins of the past. Jesus urged men and women to reach forward and grasp the good things to come. And the first of these is the assurance of divine forgiveness. It is no matter that some of those who receive the message have been publicans or harlots. The tragedy is that the self-sufficiency of Pharisees makes them heedless of the Gospel. So it is an eschatological forgiveness that Jesus preached.

It is evident that the Gospel faced its first hearers with a now-or-never decision, such as only those modern Christians experience who are abruptly converted out of irreligion or indifference. It is, however, not the psychology of the first converts but the general circumstances of their encounter with the Gospel, to which we must look for the explanation of their reception of the proferred forgiveness as eschatological. For the elements in the Gospel picture only fall into place, and begin to make sense, when it is recognized that an agelong purpose of God is working out, and that the forgiveness now offered through the Gospel is appropriate to this turning-point in the world's history.

But it proved to be inseparable from a corporate adventure of forgiven believers, towards the establishing of God's kingdom over the hearts of men. As they draw to their end, the Gospels reveal that Jesus himself, God's Word, incarnate, risen, and ascended, is that act of God in which his purpose is made clear, and has moved to the last stage before its final goal. Thus it was a forgiveness of sins in the Name of Jesus Christ, implemented by baptism into that Name, that was preached by the infant Church. Of those who answered the preaching, the Church demanded faith accompanied by moral conversion. And when these were evident, the convert was baptized and received into the fellowship, his baptism being for the total remission of his sins.

At this point the argument may suitably be supported by a summary of the section of Kittel's *Wörterbuch zum Neuen Testament* on *Aphesis hamartiōn*, forgiveness of sins. He says somewhat as follows: The expressions concerning forgiveness of sins in the Gospels are in continuity with those of the Old Testament. The specifically new thing is the looking for forgiveness as a fruit of the saving work of Christ. God is the judge to whom man is answerable. But assurance of divine forgiveness is not reached by reasoning about God's nature and attributes. It is testified as a fact of the experience of salvation; so that the preaching of forgiveness is not by exposition of theology, but by the proclamation of Good News. The context is eschatological. Accordingly, sins are not treated as so many incidents, but as all rooted in a power of evil with which God will make an end. To receive forgiveness, the sinner sides with God against the old Adam within him. Eschatological forgiveness embraces the whole future, so that it is anomalous for one who accepts it to ally himself again with evil.

Was it expected, then, of those who received this eschatological forgiveness, that they would thereafter cease from sin? The answer which the earliest Christian writings seem to testify is in the affirmative. They show us the primitive Christian community as living in an atmosphere of tense expectancy and inspired effort; as looking forward to the coming again of the Lord Jesus in glory. That was the unquestioned conviction of the first disciples, and it was rapidly communicated to ever-increasing numbers of new converts. How long would it be till the Lord came again? To this question there was no permissible answer.

Nevertheless, there was a very strong impression that the time could not be long, and that the world-order that had endured hitherto was hastening to its end. This impression seems to have continued in undiminished force for more than a decade; a fact which gives us the measure of the intensity of those experiences of the Person and resurrection of Christ which formed the matrix of Christian faith, and of the Church.

An analogy may suggest an explanation of this impression. A person who begins to feel something never experienced before will try to interpret the feeling, and the interpretation may be fantastic. But the cause of the experience will, in due course, proclaim its true meaning. What the first Christians experienced signified, not that time was running out, but that an eternal present transcends the temporal. And we must recognize that already during his ministry, the preaching of Jesus had revealed a tragic intensity of meaning in man's earthly existence, which his resurrection only confirmed and illuminated. Thus the primitive Church lived under a sense of crisis, demanding of every believer a changed life. The ethic of people living in such an atmosphere was bound to differ from any that we have known in later times. Perhaps our nearest comparable experience is that of the morale of a nation at war. There were, in the primitive Christian Church, the same stern standards of conduct that characterize a people at war. If imagination will serve us at all to enter into that atmosphere, we shall cease to be astounded by such passages as Mark 9.42, 'whosoever shall cause one of these little ones that believe on me to stumble, it were better for him if a great millstone were hanged about his neck, and he were cast into the sea.' We shall find the heroicity of primitive Christian manners reflected in the verses that follow: 'And if thy hand cause thee to stumble, cut it off; it is good for thee to enter into life maimed, rather than having thy two hands to go into hell.' It is the ethic of a last holy war for the recapture of mankind from the power of evil. And it is the sense of war to the death that provides the atmosphere in which we can rightly view the horrific picture of the deceit and death of Ananias and Sapphira (Acts 5.1–10).

Unless we make an effort of imagination to recapture the feeling of those first Christian years, in all its difference from our own, much that is written in the Gospels and Acts must seem to us grotesque. But the effort called for is not one of purely historical imagination. It is also a moral effort. For while it is a past age of which we read, it is one whose heroic standards have relevance to every Christian age.

This heroic ethic of the primitive Christians, based upon the thought that the time for which it endures will be short, and a time of crisis, has been named an interim ethic. Under this interim ethic the lapse of a Christian is surrounded with all the tragic associations of treason and cowardice in war. But the picture which Acts gives of the life of the first Christian community is not one that suggests many lapses. Rather, it seems to show us a multitude of believers who live without sinning, because, we might say, they are otherwise occupied. They are following divine guidance in a new and uplifting enterprise, upheld by the power of the Paraclete within them. It was as a forgiven people that they had received him, and as forgiven people they must retain him. Later on we shall meet with evidence of a superstitious belief in security from temptation and sin, as given by baptism. That such a belief could arise is striking testimony to the standards of life in the Church of the first age. But this belief was promptly reproved as superstition. We can be sure, therefore, that the original doctrine of baptism was that it is a sacred rite which calls men to a life, not of security and complacency, but of watchfulness and girded loins. We may gather from the Lord's Prayer that the state of being forgiven was the heart of the eschatological life. Each time that the Christian prayed that the Kingdom might come, he was to pray for himself, that he might be kept forgiven. And as the indispensable condition of the granting of that prayer, he must offer to God his pledge of forgiving all trespasses against himself. For such is the interpretation of the Prayer required by the terms of the Matthean parable of the Unmerciful Servant (18.23–34). From this it appears that the Christian's chief peril is that the Evil one should steal away the divine gift of charity from his heart.

An anonymous writer, in the second century, tried, in retrospect, to picture those first days of the Church, in a work[1] entitled *The Teaching of the Lord by the Twelve Apostles to the Gentiles*. (It is more shortly called the *Didache*.) This writer, with his eye on St Matthew, pictures the Saviour, on the eve of his ascension, commanding that Gentile converts, until more could be done for the care of their souls, should be taught to say the Lord's Prayer thrice daily. The author of the *Didache* seems to think that, by this repeated act of faith, hope, and above all charity, Christians of the primitive simplicity could be kept safe from danger of lapse into sin. In so writing, this author throws all his weight upon St Matthew, and imagines the conversion of Gentiles to begin at once after Christ's ascension. The Acts of the Apostles gives a different picture. It clearly implies an interval in which the Gospel was not preached to Gentiles. When it began to be so preached, the leaders of the Church of Christ in Israel are represented as seeing, in this conversion of Gentiles, an act of God no less astonishing than the foundation of the

[1] In *Early Christian Fathers* (Library of Christian Classics I), 1953, pp. 171–9.

Church itself. And as we are thereafter shown the Gospel spreading among the Gentiles, the apostles are represented as following the hand of God in these events. Indeed, but for the fact of this reliance upon divine guidance, we could not comprehend the reckless boldness with which baptism was granted to Gentile converts lacking all previous moral and religious preparation, upon the simple proof of their faith.

The entry of Gentiles into the Church had two important consequences. The first was that the magnitude of the evangelistic prospect that now opened before the eyes of the disciples was such as to modify eschatological expectations; not, indeed, in substance (for it was still believed that those were the last times), but in regard to the length of time to be passed before the coming again of Christ. The other consequence was to modify the supposition that the baptized Christian would no more transgress the moral law. That a Christian should turn back to the world about to perish, and enter again into servitude to the Evil one, remained something fearful and catastrophic. But baptized Gentiles, however wonderfully changed by their conversion, were seen easily to transgress the revealed moral laws, through ignorance and lack of training. They needed correction; perhaps admonishing. But their transgression did not merit removal from the Church. It was in fact the undesired survival of old life-habits, now mortally stricken, although not actually dead. Besides this, the eschatological context of the Gospel was new to these Gentile converts, as it was not for the converts of Israel.

Certainly we see the Gospel preached in an eschatological context at Thessalonica. But St Paul was plainly very anxious whether the Thessalonian converts, who were in need of so much instruction, would remain steady. When, however, he received good news of them, he took courage, and renewed his hope that they would be preserved blameless unto the coming of the Lord. He directed (II Thess. 3.14f) that brethren who went back upon the faith they had received should be put out of the Church. If, however, they were led to make their submission, it would prove that their disobedience had not been wilful sin after baptism, but only the momentary failure of a faith imperfectly formed. Here, and at Corinth, we see St Paul remarkably gentle towards departures from the Christian way of life on the part of Gentile converts. And it is no wonder, in such circumstances, that the leaders of Jewish Christianity took alarm, and that some urged that Gentiles should be trained as proselytes, before they were baptized. This proposal brought St Paul to bay, so soon as it threatened the status of his first Galatian churches. He claimed that Christians are under no law but the law of the fruits of the Spirit, who is given in answer to faith alone. Nevertheless, in Gal. 6.1, he admits the possibility of brethren being surprised into transgression of that law. He appeals, in that event, to his true disciples, who walk by the Spirit, to help restore such undeliberately lapsed brethren. The pointed addressing of this appeal to the *pneumatici* (spiritual men) implies that the legalistic among the brethren would act differently. They would, in short, acknowledge no ecclesiastical pardon to be possible, of those convicted of post-baptismal sin.

We hear the genuine voice of Israelite Christianity in the Epistle to the Hebrews, with its classical expression in 10.26, 'For if we sin wilfully after that we have received the knowledge of the truth, there remaineth no more a sacrifice for sins, but a certain fearful expectation of judgement'. Together with this go the sombre verses which follow, about Christians who 'tread under foot the Son of the God', and so relapse, without hope of recovery, under the dreadful judgment of the living God.

These words were written a long while after St Paul's Epistle to the Galatians, and show how little the discussion of the relation of Gentiles to the law had led to any general tolerance towards the sinning of Christians after baptism.

The position which St Paul took up in that Epistle, he established, with all deliberation, in the seventh chapter of his Epistle to the Romans. There we have the picture of a Christian in whose mortal body the law of sin is still regnant, even though, with his true personal will, he is battling for sinlessness. At Corinth, on the other hand, St Paul met the troubles of an apostle to Gentiles in their full force, and learned, by bitter experience, that the natural law of conscience, which he extolled, in Romans, as a guide to the Gentiles, did not suffice to prevent his Corinthian Greeks from mistaking licence for the liberty of the Spirit. He had, accordingly, to draw up a list of behaviours incompatible with Christian faith, and to impose it upon the Corinthians in the manner of a new code of law, to which he attached the discipline of excommunication (I Cor. 5.11). In II Cor. 2, we have evidence that this discipline led to the restoration of a grievous offender. But the close of the Epistle shows that a situation of crisis still remained. Thus we cannot find, in these Epistles, the surrender in principle of the expectation that a baptized member of Christ's Church must live blameless until the Lord come.

If such a surrender had taken place, St Paul must have told his Gentile converts to confess, repent and seek a new forgiveness for the reappearance of the old Adam in the lives which caused him such pastoral concern, This he did not do; since to have done so would have been to allow these Christians to acquiesce in the recrudescence of their old life. That was clearly not his mind.

If the General Epistle of St James is to be numbered among the older books of the New Testament, it presents all the more striking a contrast with St Paul's Epistles to the Corinthians. Addressed, as it seems to be, to Judaeo-Christians who have come to their new allegiance with a minimum of change in their general circumstances of life, the argument is designed to convict them of continuing in sin. These Christians regard themselves as the élite of mankind, God's firstfruits out of his creation, and on their way to perfection. But St James enumerates several ways in which, without deliberation, these would-be perfect men slip into sin, and begin to be upon a downward slope. So he ends (5.14–19) by counselling that, at the possible approach of death, the Christian should take thought whether he is fit for the world to come, and should appeal for the help of the Church, by calling to him the elders. So St James advises confession of sins, and finally pronounces the blessedness of those who are the means of recalling a brother from sin. It appears, therefore, that St James believes that, among these law-abiding Jewish Christians, many continue to sin. But he believes that there is power in the Church to aid such sinners, and not leave them to perdition.

The books of the New Testament that are certainly among the younger ones register a slight change of ground, compared with those that are older. In I Peter the possibility, at least, of Christian transgression is envisaged, since the Epistle sets out a very careful pattern of Christian conduct, and exhorts the keeping of it. In 4.7, the approaching end of the present world-order is presented as an incentive to charity, which is described as covering the multitude of sins, a phrase already encountered in the Epistle of St James. And there is insistence upon the ceaseless activity of the devil, as reason for Christians passing the time of their earthly sojourning with fear. There is, in short, a change of tone, compared with the earlier writings, which perhaps reflects the experience of the Church in the intervening years.

Before the end of the first Christian century, we find, outside the canon of Scripture, a like chastened attitude towards the expectation of Christian sinlessness that meets us in I Peter. This is in the *Epistle of Clement of Rome to the Corinthians*.[1] Clement says (51.3), that to make confession concerning our transgressions saves us from the hardening of the heart that overtook Korah, Dathan, and Abiram, who presumed upon their sanctity. We are prepared, therefore, to meet, as we do in more than one early second century document, reference to the making of confession of sins by Christians when beginning prayer. But in none of these contexts can it safely be concluded that anything more is implied than a humble acknowledgment of frailty based upon a recollection of prebaptismal sins.

Whatever opinion is held as to the date and circumstances of composition of the Pastoral Epistles, it will be agreed that they testify to the later state of congregations that remained in the Pauline tradition, In spite of arguments that have been put forward to the contrary, it is still possible to date them in St Paul's lifetime and to treat their text as, in the main, authentically his work. They may be, in short, just what they appear to be. In any case, the congregations in Asia and Crete to which these letters refer are shown as held together by dint of a strong exercise of pastorate, now deputed by the apostle to lieutenants. A word characteristic of this pastorate (and indeed of the epistles) is *elenchein*, meaning to bring home to someone a moral truth which he has failed to observe. The people who are being held in Christian communion, in these churches, need such handling. It is necessary to call men from the congregations to take part in the work of local pastorate. Candidates have to be selected with great care, and even after they have taken office, it may have to

[1] In *Early Christian Fathers* (Library of Christian Classics I), 1953, pp. 43–73.

be brought home to them that they are sinning (so I Tim. 5.20). This might entail removal from office, or even excommunication; in which case 5.22 may refer to a rite for their restoration, though one not lightly to be granted, as the apostle makes clear. The general position in these Pauline churches seems to be that, as long as believers will submit to pastorate, they can be held in the company of the forgiven. There is a background in which we discern others who go their own way, and must be let go. Willingness to submit to pastoral discipline *ipso facto* calls in question the deliberateness of the offence, and so the situation that confronts us here is not materially different from that which was before us in Gal. 6.1.

There are, however, no traces of long survival, in the life of the early Church, of these Pauline missionary methods, of founding churches almost within a period of hours, and then shaping them to the Christian pattern by the exertions of missionary superintendents. And this fact should warn us not to suppose that the picture of Gentile congregations given us in the earlier Pauline epistles is fully typical of congregations that were rapidly multiplying round the Mediterranean during the later first century. St Paul was a unique figure in the Church of his time, and the Pauline pattern of Gentile Church life probably did not long survive the apostle. A main reason for this may well have been that a compromise was presently reached between Pauline practice and the Judaizing plan for making proselytes of Gentile converts to Christianity. This compromise was by the adoption, in the Gentile churches, of a lengthy catechumenate, or period of training and instruction before baptism. The training was for life under the New Covenant, but perhaps it owed something of its character to the training of proselytes under the Old.

A special interest attaches to the group of New Testament

books which bear the name of John. It is conjectured that these all come from one area, Asia Minor, and one period, beginning not earlier than the last decade of the first Christian century. It may be judged, further, that the Christian communities of which they are representative were not in close touch with those other Christian communities of the Mediterranean lands, such as the churches in Rome, Antioch, Corinth, and Caesarea in Palestine, in which the other New Testament books were first current. The most likely reasons for such a temporary isolation of the 'John' churches are their fear of heresy, and the impact upon them of local persecution. Thus John the Seer seems to see the whole battle for the true faith as concentrated in seven congregations, now threatened with a renewal of persecution, in the Province of Asia. If this means that the 'John' churches felt themselves to be standing alone, there is the less ground for surprise at the individuality of outlook shown in the 'John' writings. This individuality is particularly marked in their divergence from the eschatological preoccupations that appear in the other New Testament books. In the Johannine Gospel, the prince of this world is already judged (16.11), and that even before the cruci-fixion. Further, while Christ's work in the Church is to continue, by the present help of the Paraclete, until the Lord comes again, the appendix to the Gospel expressly discounts the expectation of the end coming within the lifetime of the last survivor of the Twelve. Nevertheless, the emphasis laid, in this Gospel, upon the new birth of those who receive the baptism of water and of the Spirit, suggests that the evangelist expected true Christians to continue without sin.

The John of the Catholic Epistles, on the other hand, is quite explicit in his statement that Christians *have* sin (I John 1.8–10). That clearly means more than that they sinned formerly. And it is in regard to these sins which they have, being Christians, that 'John' says that Jesus Christ the righteous is their propitiation (2.2). The authority for saying that Christians sin, it appears, is a *logos* (reasoned statement) of Christ. It cannot be said whether this *logos* was a particular saying, or whether the reference is to the general tenor of Christ's teaching. But it causes our author to say that, so far from a Christian being anathema if he has to confess to post-baptismal sin, he is anathema if he denies it. Nevertheless, 'John' still expects that Christians, by abiding in Christ, will remain sinless; for he says (3.4–7), 'Sin is lawlessness. And ye know that Christ was manifested to take away sins, and in him is no sin. Whosoever abideth in him sinneth not . . . (9) Whosoever is begotten of God doeth no sin; because his seed abideth in him: and he cannot sin, because he is begotten of God'. The paradox on the sinless who sin is resolved in the writer's recognition that there are two categories of sinning, where Christians are concerned. One category is sin unto death (I John 5.16f). With regard to lapses of that kind, 'John' approves rigorism. The brethren must hold anathema the baptized person whose sin thus cancels his seeming faith in Christ. But if they discern that the sin of the Christian in question is not a sin unto death, they are to pray for him, and their intercession will gain for him release from the spiritual death that otherwise would follow sin. Thus this writer makes the life of Christians one in which they go on seeking the sinlessness of which Christ himself is their assurance, though they do not fully, in this age, attain that which they seek.

Of John the Seer, the first thing to note is that he reverts to a form of apocalyptic that flourished in Israel before Christ. He interprets the moral gloom of the world in which the Church is bearing her witness as signifying that these are the last times, much as do the writers of earlier Jewish apocalyptic. In this respect, the John of the Catholic Epistles stands close to him.

The other fact about John the Seer that calls for notice is that, authorized by a vision of the glorified Christ, in the midst of a crisis of persecution, he sounds a call to a new penitence. This call is addressed to churches of baptized Christians.

So, putting together the impressions to be gathered from the younger New Testament writings, we seem to see that, as the first Christian century reached its close, many had come to recognize that the Christian life, while it must ever cling to the pursuit of sinlessness, needed still, and that on account of post-baptismal sins, to be a penitent life. We should gather that these sins of the baptized, while undoubtedly calling for divine forgiveness, were not such as forthwith to extinguish in the sinner the grace of faith. In the matter of this modification of the primitive Christian expectation of sinlessness, the 'John' churches appear as more advanced than the other Mediterranean churches.

A light is thrown upon this movement away from rigorism by a letter[1] of the younger Pliny to the emperor Trajan, written about AD 112. Pliny had been sent as Legate to Bithynia, to deal with a state of unrest prevailing in the province. He found the province 'riddled', as he conceived it, with Christianity. He assumed that Christianity was something subversive. Nevertheless, he endeavoured to discover for himself its true nature. The evidence which he obtained that seemed to him the most enlightening came from a number of people who admitted to having been Christians, but who said that they had left off (*se desinisse*), being Christians at various times, up to as long as twenty years previously. Their evidence showed no hostility or vindictiveness towards the faith that they had abandoned. On the con-

[1] Epistle X. 96, in G. B. Allen, *Pliny's Letters*, 2nd ed., 1924, pp. 64–6.

CHAPTER TWO

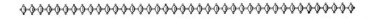

The Preaching of Second Repentance

AVAILABLE evidence does not entitle us to suppose that the Johannine writings had become the possession of the whole catholic Church before AD 150 at the earliest. A little before this date, and without sign of influence from I John or the Apocalypse, two writings appeared in Mediterranean churches of apostolic foundation, which testify that the sins of Christians had begun to be felt there as an acute problem. Both writings are in Greek. One of them certainly emanates from Rome. The place of origin of the other is more problematical. Which appeared first and whether one was influenced by the other are disputed questions. Most likely they were independent expressions of a wave of concern over falling standards of sanctity in the Church, felt by many Christian congregations round the Mediterranean. The shorter and simpler of these writings has come down in manuscript tradition under the title of Clement of Rome's *Second Epistle to the Corinthians*.[1] But contents and style show it to be neither by Clement nor an epistle; they show it, in fact, to be a sermon, prepared in writing, and delivered in the church congregation. The preacher, who makes no pretensions to literary style, and phrases his message too unassumingly to have been a bearer of the highest order of official responsibility, would seem to be one of the presbyters of the church he is addressing. We may gather that it had fallen to him to deliver the homily

[1] In *Early Christian Fathers* (Library of Christian Classics I), 1953, pp. 193–202.

on this occasion. He seems to allude (19.1) to the expectation of receiving a reward from the congregation for his sermon, in preparation of which he had clearly been at great pains. He calls it an 'appeal', and says that the reward which he desires to receive from them is that they will repent from their hearts, and so, at the same time, reward themselves with life and salvation. He pleads with them to repent now, while there is opportunity, for, he assures them, after this life there will be no more opportunity to confess or repent.

It is clear, therefore, that this was no routine sermon. This unknown presbyter took his opportunity to lay bare a crisis in the history of the congregation. A gulf has opened between the ideal and the actual, so that even the outside world can see that Christians are not living up to the level of the teachings of Christ. So he exclaims (13.1), 'Let us now repent, and awake to the good, for we are simply full of stupidity and badness.' This would be a counsel of despair if the rigorists were right. But our preacher sees hope in repenting. For he has a new eschatology, which he derives from an apocryphal Gospel. This Gospel contained a cryptic prophecy on the part of the Saviour that he will come again when there awaits him on earth, as a bride adorned for her husband, a truly sanctified Church. In other words, our author believes that the return of Christ in glory is being delayed by the tepidity of Christians, so that he conceives himself to be sounding a call to the Church to awake and 'take the Kingdom by storm'. If this call is directly to his own congregation or by implication to all congregations at that moment in history, his notion of the Church extends far beyond the actuality of the moment. The Church is, for him, a timeless concept in the mind of God.

This seems to our preacher to place the actual Church in the same place as was held before by Israel, so that the promises of God in the Old Testament can be fully appropriated by Christians. So the parable of the potter, in Jeremiah 18, gives hope that the marring of the Church by the sins of her members may yet be put right by the reformation of her members. But as the misshapen pot cannot be reshaped after it has been fired, so the Christian sinner's hope of reformation and a place in the sanctified Church, lies in his repentance while still living in the flesh[1] (8.2). An additional inducement to respond to the appeal is provided by the thought of setting the right standards before the young people growing up in the Christian society (19.1), who, in their turn, will further sanctify the Bride of Christ, and thus hasten the Lord's coming again.

Logically, this part of the argument would seem to open the way to an indefinite number of Christian repentances. But our preacher presents what seems a once-for-all appeal, to be answered by repentance now, with nothing to suggest that it is not a final repentance. It is implied that it is a very drastic repentance, such as the Seer of the Apocalypse demanded from the churches of Asia. The preacher calls for a fresh renunciation of this present world, expressing itself in costly self-discipline, fasting, prayer and, above all (as striking at the roots of the hold which this world is gaining over Christians), the unstinting giving of alms. His appeal sets before his hearers the choice of heaven or hell.

So simple and unstudied is the presentation of the theme, that we may reasonably see, in this sermon, a first official broaching, in that congregation, of the need and possibility of Second Repentance within the Church. In this case, the sermon made history, and its survival is so far explained.

As to date, this sermon can be placed, with fair certainty, in

[1] Cf. Luke 16.26 and Nemesius (Library of Christian Classics IV, 1955, p. 244).

the fourth decade of the second Christian century. It must be after AD 132, when Hadrian's suppression of the Jewish revolt so changed the relative numerical strength of Judaism and Christianity that, for the first time, it became possible for Christians to think, as our preacher does, that Christians now outnumber Jews (2.3). On the other hand, his loose way of citing New Testament writings, and his trustful acceptance of an apocryphal Gospel, is hardly consistent with a date lower than, say, AD 140.

It was known in Corinth, in the middle second century, that the famous epistle they had received from the Roman church had Clement as author. There is no reason to suppose that this fact was generally known. If, therefore, it was in the church archives of Corinth that our sermon was preserved, next after the Roman epistle, the supposition that it was a second epistle of Clement to the Corinthians might be explained. Such a supposition might be helped by the fact that in *I Clement* 63.2 the Epistle is named an 'appeal', as our sermon is designated in *II Clement* 19.1. What may be an allusion to the Isthmian Games, in our sermon (ch. 7), affords another reason for thinking that it may have been preached in Corinth.

This general fact, as touching the outlook of second century Christians, emerges from our study of this document. The days of interim ethic were past. Instead of expecting to see the return of Christ with the eyes of their flesh, Christians now expected to die without having seen it. It follows that a new Christian ethic, of preparation for the after-life, replaced the earlier interim ethic. And the preacher of *II Clement* saw that this involved the possibility of reconversion. And we must attribute to the continuing influence of the older ethic the fact that, at this stage, reconversion could only be envisaged as once-for-all reconversion, or Second Repentance.

Around the middle of the second century, the subject of penance in the Church was treated much more elaborately in a work emanating from the Roman church, entitled *The Shepherd of Hermas*.[1] This work rapidly extended its influence among the Mediterranean churches, so as to seem likely, for a while, to be accorded a place among the canonical Scriptures of the New Testament. This fact is sufficient proof that the theme of post-baptismal sin was claiming the concern of Christians far and wide. The book purports to record the spiritual adventures of a lay member of the Roman church named Hermas. It opens with a slight framework of autobiography, followed by a circumstantial account of five visions, in the last of which Hermas comes face to face with an angel dressed as a shepherd, who has been sent to instruct him concerning penance. This figure explains the title of the book. From the angelic pastor Hermas receives twelve moral instructions, prescribing right courses of conduct, and for this reason called Commandments. The rest of the book is formed of eight doctrinal Parables, which Hermas is represented as hearing from the angel, or seeing enacted, under his guidance.

Like the author of *II Clement*, Hermas has a new eschatology. Christ is building a tower, his 'temple not made with hands', and the stones are elect souls, perfected in the trials and temptations of this present world. In this temple, when it is completed, he will come again. It is a like conception to that in the English funeral collect, in its petition 'that it may please thee, of thy gracious goodness, shortly to accomplish the number of thine elect, and to hasten thy kingdom'. That phrase was no doubt inspired by the Apocalypse, dominated by the notion of a sacred number. The idea, as it appears in Hermas, of the completion of

[1] In *The Apostolic Fathers* (Ante-Nicene Christian Library I), 1867, pp. 323–75, or in *Excluded books of the New Testament*, J. B. Lightfoot etc., 1927.

a purpose, is more typical of a Western writing. *The Shepherd* has been the subject of very thorough literary study, the results of which are brought together by M. Dibelius, in the Supplementary Volume of Lietzmann's *Handbuch zum Neuen Testament* devoted to New Testament apocrypha (1923). The first thing established is the literary artificiality of the work. The author has taken his model from those prophetical books of the Old Testament that combine narrative and prophecy. But the construction of his book has been a work of thorough-going plagiarism. He has apparently raided a whole library of works otherwise lost to us, of which some were pagan, some came from the circle of the liberal synagogue, and some were Christian. He joined his borrowings together very loosely, as though he were much more preoccupied with the over-all result than with the style of presentation. There can be no doubt that his main purpose was to neutralize the rigorism, with regard to post-baptismal sin, traditional in the Church. It is equally clear that he succeeded remarkably in this aim. For, in the wake of the diffusion of *The Shepherd*, there appears, all round the Mediterranean, public recognition of penance undertaken by Christians in the Church for sins committed since baptism. The influence of the book was doubtless enhanced by the fact that it was everywhere accepted at its face value, as a work of Christian prophecy.

In view of the model upon which the author has shaped his book, we shall not expect to find an argument developed step by step in logical order. It is plain, nevertheless, that the Visions, in presenting studies of the subtle infiltration of evil into the mind, of the spiritual distractions that arise from life in the world, and of the trouble of a devout mind when burdened in conscience, prepares the reader to look favourably upon the plea of the Christian sinner for a renewal of hope. But only in the middle of the Fourth Commandment is Hermas made to put to the angel pastor the question upon which everything depends, 'Is there hope for the Christian sinner in a second repentance?' This takes place in the following dialogue:

H. I have heard, Sir, from certain teachers, that there is no other repentance than that one when we went down into the water, and received remission of our former sins.

A. You have heard correctly. For so it is. He who has received remission of sin ought never to sin again, but to live blamelessly. But since you press me for the whole truth, I will tell you; though what I say does not apply to those to be baptized in days to come, nor to the latest company of neophytes. For these last, as likewise those that come after, have remission of former sins in their baptism, but after that no more repenting of sins. The Second Repentance which the Lord appoints is for people who were baptized before the present time. For the Lord knows what is in the heart, and foreknows all things. Known to him were the infirmity of men and the cunning of the devil; and how that the devil would do some evil to the servants of God, in leading them to sin. Therefore the Lord, being full of compassion, had mercy on his creatures, and for their sakes has appointed, under my hand, this call to repentance. And I declare to you that if, after that great and solemn calling (in baptism), a man be tempted by the devil, and sin, he has ONE opportunity of repentance. But if he sin repeatedly, repentance shall not profit him. It will go hard if such a man shall live.

H. You have given me fresh life, by this clear declaration, giving me the assurance that, if I add no more to my sin, I may be saved.

A. You, and all who do likewise, shall be saved. (IV.3.1–6).

In this passage, rigorism is challenged, upon the authority of a prophetic revelation, but it is caused to give only a little ground. The indulgence granted by the angel pastor of Hermas is to a single Christian generation, and does not extend into the future. Nevertheless it is plain that the actual effect, as well as the apparent aim, of the book as a whole, was to open Second Repentance to Christians for all time. Is the limitation imposed in this dialogue reflected in the rest of the book? A negative answer is given by Father Joseph Grotz, S.J. in *Die Entwicklung des Bussstufenwesens in der vornicaenischen Kirche* (Freiburg i/B, 1955) in the course of a detailed study of Vision III, and Parables VIII and IX. These passages are interpreted by Father Grotz as not only recognizing penance in the Church, but as outlining an elaborate casuistry answering to different sorts and degrees of post-baptismal sin. These passages could therefore only have been written long after that situation represented in the dialogue of Commandment IV could have been actual, in the Roman church. These observations suggest a possible solution to the problem of the literary history of *The Shepherd*. The Christian prophet Hermas may be a historical figure, but belonging to the end of the first century and the age of Clement. His claim to a revelation that certain contemporary Christians were to be retained in the communion of the Church, on condition of renewed conversion, may have effected the first breach in the rigorist front. We may then suppose that the Roman church proceeded, from this start, to recognize the right of various categories of post-baptismal sinner to remain in communion on condition of doing penance. Other persons may have been held out of communion, some for a time, and some for life. It goes without saying that Christians who sinned and did not repent, were held to be lost, alike to the Church and to the hope of final salvation. Those who fell away again after doing penance, and some whose sins were of a particularly heinous kind, may have been admitted to the church gathering, but to be dismissed, together with the hearers, without hope of restoration to the communion of the empirical Church. They could, however, count upon the continual intercession of the Church on their behalf. And so they might have hope that, by perseverance in faith and penitence, they would attain salvation in the world to come. In the middle of the second century, after such a history, we can understand an anonymous author composing a 'Prophecy of Hermas' which might be better described as artificial, than as fictitious. We shall then see the work in our hands as covering the whole rationale of Christian penance, as it was ordered in the mid-second century in the Roman church. And if this is how *The Shepherd* came to be written, the Muratorian Canon must be judged right in describing it as 'recent', but probably wrong in fathering it upon the Hermas who was brother to Pope Pius I.

The high honour in which the Epistle to the Hebrews was, on the testimony of *I Clement*, held in the Roman church must have given support to the rigorist tradition there, so that progress towards the recognition of Second Repentance is likely to have been by small stages. Roman Christians were evidently living under the shadow cast by Heb. 6.1–5 and 10.26. And that is exactly what we read between the lines of *The Shepherd*. As to the manner of the Christian penance disclosed in *The Shepherd*, we can only gather that the Christian of burdened conscience declared himself as a penitent in the liturgical gathering and removed from his accustomed place among the faithful to a recognised inferior place. This step, we should gather, was voluntary and might as well be undertaken out of tenderness of conscience as on account of special guilt. It seems to have been only in certain scandalous cases that the sinner was driven to penance by threat of excommunication. Some such sinners (such as those who were intimidated into hiding or denying their faith) seem to have been warned that if they delayed to do penance, they would be put out of communion. However, there is nothing in *The Shepherd* to suggest that those who did voluntary penance lost thereby the privilege of communion. On the other hand, penance clearly involved a reconversion so drastic that, if further repenting were ever needful, the Second Repentance would be regarded as spurious. Even when that happened, however, it was not the end of all hope of salvation, although it removed all hope of further communion with the empirical Church. Father Grotz points out that, towards the end of our dialogue from the Fourth Commandment, it is not said that the backslider from penance is lost, but only that it will go hard with him not to be lost. That means that he will be lost unless he perseveres till death, as a penitent frequenting the first part of the liturgy, but excluded from communion.

The conclusion to which this chapter leads is that the churches of the Mediterranean entered the second century bound by a rigorist doctrine of Christian sanctity, which saw no alternative to refusing communion to Christians found to have fallen into serious sin after baptism. But during the first half of the century a widespread movement took place in favour of recognizing a single opportunity of post-baptismal penance. It was accepted as beyond question that the conscience-stricken Christian must take prompt and drastic steps to sever the ties of affection holding him to this present world. The love of property, and of fleshly comfort and pleasure, was regarded as being the heart of the danger, and, at this worldly affection, Second Repentance must strike without mercy. And, at least according to the Roman view,

Second Repentance must be, no less than baptism, a once-for-all and unrepeatable act on the part of the penitent.

But the acknowledgement of Second Repentance betokened no change in doctrine with regard to the forgiven life. Irenaeus, in his *Proof of the Apostolic Preaching*,[1] in mentioning the judgment that will come upon a believer who sins (ch. 8), cites Rom. 2.4 in a way that suggests that he has the possibility of Second Repentance in view. He also has a theory of baptismal regeneration that supports the expectation of sinlessness to follow. For he says that the soul of the believer undergoes, in baptism, a resurrection whereby it is restored to its body in a new partnership, and retains the indwelling of the Spirit so long as it holds to truth.

It is plain from these passages and from others in his work *Against Heresies*[2] that Irenaeus looked for some very palpable change in the moral life of the baptized to follow baptism, which would render sinlessness possible, where before it was impossible. With this belief accords his insistence upon the ecclesiastical tradition, and the very thorough catechesis whereby candidates for baptism were put in possession of the faith and Christian way of life. Under these circumstances, there was good reason for insisting that the remission of sins would be sought in vain outside the Catholic Church, in which alone the pure tradition of Christian faith and life are maintained. It calls for some exercise of imagination on the part of the modern Christian to picture the changed and committed outlook of the second century convert who had attained to baptism by so exacting and formative a course of instruction and training. The candidate himself was drawn into making a threefold response of repentance, faith, and

---

[1] *Proof of the Apostolic Preaching* (Ancient Christian Writers 16), 1952.
[2] In *The Writings of Irenaeus*, 2 vols. (Ante-Nicene Christian Library V), 1868.

CHAPTER THREE

The Practice of Second Repentance

BY the time that the second century drew to its close, we have two-fold evidence of the influence exerted by *The Shepherd of Hermas* south of the Mediterranean. This comes from Alexandria, in the writings of Titus Flavius Clemens (Clement of Alexandria), and from Carthage, in those of Quintus Septimius Florens Tertullianus (Tertullian). It is not, perhaps, a mere coincidence that both writers, as their names might indicate, should belong to the upper or official ranks of society. For, in *The Shepherd*, the need for Second Repentance is much associated with the clinging of Christians, after conversion, to their possessions, and to their place in the life of the present age. Parable 9.20 says that those who cling to the life of the present age do not cleave to the Church, and that it is difficult for the rich so to do, because they have to fear that, in the Church, they will meet demands to help the poor, out of their wealth. In this passage we may, perhaps, discern the inspiration of the tract which Clement of Alexandria wrote, under the title *Who is the rich man that is being saved?*[1] We know, from Clement's *Stromateis* (Lectures on Christian life and doctrine), that he himself must have been a man of means. It is possible that this tract, which, by its directness, is in such contrast of style with Clement's lectures, belongs to his first literary activity. He shows himself

---

[1] In *Clement of Alexandria* (Loeb Classical Library), 1919.

primarily concerned to lessen the inducements to hold back from
baptism, which worked upon those wealthy persons who were
attracted to the Christian faith. Clement has first to dispose of
their fear that, if they were baptized, they would have to denude
themselves of their rank and possessions. Clement is aware that
Christ's words about the rich young enquirer (Mark 10.17–31)
might seem to justify that fear. He says, therefore, that if it is so
interpreted, it demeans our Lord to plagiarizing from the Cynics.
The spiritual meaning of 'sell whatsoever thou hast', he says, is
'wean your soul from the love of possession'. So baptism simply
pledges the rich man to become the steward of his possessions, instead of being their slave. Of course the rich Christian will meet
with calls upon his generosity, but the alms-roll of the church will
provide him with clients who will be bedesmen and intercessors
for him. In allusion to our Lord's prayer for Peter (Luke 22.31f),
Clement tells the rich man, 'One of your bedesmen will be able
to make request for you with God'. If there is also allusion to
I John 5.16, Clement's thought is that, even before the patron has
sinned a sin not unto death, the bedesman's prayer will be guard-
ing him from temptation. So Clement paints an attractive picture
of the life of the rich man turned Christian. But now he has to
meet the other fear of the man of social position, when he contemplates baptism. This is that he will prove unable to fulfil the
requirements of the forgiven life. Clement does not make light of
this difficulty. His words (Ch. 39) are, 'Suppose that, by any
chance, through ignorance, infirmity or circumstance, and without meaning to, he were to tumble, after his sealing and redemption, into certain sins or transgressions, so as to go into a fatal
decline, why then he must fall under the total condemnation of
God.'

Perhaps we may regard this as a deliberate overstatement, to make way for what follows. Clement even darkens the picture in Ch. 40, by saying that the task of the Christian is to cut off passions that have grown up with him. Now this is just the consideration which weighed upon persons who enjoyed the privileges of wealth and position in Graeco-Roman society. But against all these difficulties, Clement now invokes the considerations on the other side; the grace of God, the intercession of the brethren, the possibilities that lie in sincere repentance, and in perseverance in the effort to live aright. So he commends Second Repentance, but in a form appropriate to the rich. For what he proposes is a literal translation of the angel-pastor of Hermas into flesh and blood. In Ch. 41, he tells the rich penitent to take a 'trainer and director', provided from among those who depend upon the alms of the church, to live in his house, as the intimate companion of his private life. Clement is evidently anxious to give his hypothetical rich penitent every confidence in the ability of such a 'private chaplain', backed by the prayers of the whole congregation, to bring his penance to a happy conclusion. And so he relates, in the last chapter (42), a story about the apostle St John, that he pursued a young Christian who had, after baptism, fallen into bad company and become leader of a gang of bandits, to their stronghold. There he won back the young man to Christ, swearing to him that he should receive remission of the sins he had committed since his baptism. This story, as Clement narrates it, has all the marks of a piece of popular hagiology. Clement, who, before he settled at Alexandria about AD 180, had travelled widely for the purpose of visiting Christian teachers of note, may be presumed to have come across it in the country of the 'John' churches. After the typical manner of Christian legend, it exaggerates the moral of I John 5.16. But in the eyes of Clement, it demonstrates, by an argument *a fortiori*, that the way of post-baptismal penance is not a lonely way, but that the sympathy and intercession of brethren afford both aid and encouragement to those who have to tread it.

Tertullian has something to tell us with regard to the practice of Second Repentance in his work *On Penitence*,[1] written not later than the opening years of the third century. In it he does not refer to *The Shepherd*, but the work *On Prayer*,[1] of about the same date, does refer to it, in terms that indicate that, at this time, Tertullian regarded *The Shepherd* as having some degree of authority. The purpose of the work *On Penitence* is so far the same as that of *The Shepherd*, as that it aims at moving Christians of burdened conscience to take the daunting step of entering upon Second Repentance. Also, Tertullian here sets before us an established form of public entry upon Second Repentance, to which he gives the Greek name of *exomologesis* (confession). Like 'Hermas', Tertullian emphasizes alike the reality of sins of thought, and the enormity of post-baptismal sin. But he detects, as 'Hermas' does not, an occasion of such sin in the reception of baptism after a false or imperfect first repentance. This is the less surprising, in view of the fact that the African churches were the fruit of something approaching a mass-conversion. Under such circumstances, rigorism could not be successfully maintained.

To commend Second Repentance, Tertullian sought for less arguable support than that of *The Shepherd* and found it in the Letters to the Seven Churches in the Apocalypse: for that book was now established as part of the canonical New Testament. Tertullian will, no doubt, have understood these letters to be summoning the backsliders whom they reprove to public penance. The rite of *exomologesis*, to which Tertullian provides this scriptural support, is an act of self-humiliation by the penitent,

[1] *On Penitence*, Ancient Christian Writers 28, 1959; *On Prayer*, E. Evans, 1953.

calculated to win the compassion of the congregation. The penitent already sleeps in sackcloth, dresses in rags, feeds little and austerely, and spends long hours in deprecatory prayer. To encourage him, Tertullian has said that God leaves the gate of forgiveness ajar, so that the Christian sinner can find the means of obtaining forgiveness, Second Repentance, in the vestibule. This figure of speech seems to hint at the actual rite of *exomologesis*, for the vestibule of the house of liturgical gathering is the place where the penitent makes public his need of penance. As the brethren arrive for the liturgy, he prostrates himself at the feet of the presbyters, kneels to 'confessors' (those who have steadfastly borne persecution) and begs the intercession of all who enter.

What, we must wonder, could supply such a sense of urgency as to bring people voluntarily to face such an ordeal? The consideration that Tertullian urges, with all his powers, is that of the pains of hell. It would seem that, when the other world had come to seem less near at hand than it did in the first Christian generation, it was felt expedient to impress its character more vividly upon the imagination of believers. For it is at this period that the fear of hell begins to figure as a preacher's theme. But Tertullian, when he has, by this means, moved his addressees to the publication of their shame, and the enlistment of the intercession of the church, leaves them with just this one hope, that by persevering to the end they may attain to eternal salvation. The implication is that they had been brought into peril by loving this world and its goods too well.

The practice which Tertullian thus describes is clearly no invention of his, but something that has prevailed for some time. The Greek title suggests that it did not originate in Africa, but had been introduced there from across the Mediterranean. For the African Church was entirely Latin-speaking. The only centre

D

in the West where we know that Greek was still being used in Christian writings into the third century was Rome. It is possible therefore that Tertullian's *exomologesis* was the spread of something that had been developing in Rome since the days of *The Shepherd of Hermas*.

This title, *exomologesis*, might suggest that the penitent made public confession of his sins, as well as begging the intercession of the brethren. Against this is the use of the corresponding verb in the Septuagint, which would seem to lay the emphasis upon the admission of having sinned, rather than upon the detailed acknowledgement of sins. It is used of confession to God in privacy, and it goes with an acknowledgement of the righteousness of God within the covenant which the human sinner has broken. Tertullian goes to the Old Testament for an example of *exomologesis* as a divine ordinance, and finds it in the punishment of Nebuchadnezzar (Dan. 4.28–34). But here no verbal confession is placed upon the lips of the offending monarch. The character of his *exomologesis* is that of a humiliation, expiating and correcting his failure to give God the glory. We should be wise, therefore, to read no more into the rite described by Tertullian than that it constituted in itself a confession of post-baptismal sin. If the rite took place literally in the vestibule, no more detailed confession would be possible or appropriate.

At a date within a year or two before AD 180, a pagan critic of Christianity called Celsus, writing very probably from Rome, launched an attack upon the new faith in a work entitled *The true doctrine*. This contains a criticism of the Christian teaching on humility, in the course of which he says that the Christian 'humble man humiliates himself in a degrading and undignified manner, throwing himself headlong to the ground upon his knees, cloth-

---

[1] See *Origen, Contra Celsum*, (translated with notes) H. Chadwick, 1953.

ing himself in beggar's rags and heaping dust upon himself.' This description (*Contra Celsum* VI.15) of behaviour tallies so well with Tertullian's rite of *exomologesis* that we may assume that it was of this rite that Celsus had gained some knowledge. But instead of taking it to be a rite, he saw in it only a typical demonstration of the Christian notion of humility. When Origen, some fifty years later, set himself to reply to Celsus, he did not recognize, in this passage, a description of Second Repentance. The explanation may be that, in the interval, the manner of entering upon Second Repentance had been mitigated.

All our evidence, from 'Hermas', Celsus, Clement of Alexandria and Tertullian, is about what the penitent Christian did when he recognized his need of Second Repentance. All the initiative seems to lie with him. Penance is an *operatio*, a spiritual labour which he undertakes in the hope that fidelity in its performance will render him forgivable. On Father Grotz's showing, some Roman church members received notice that, unless they undertook penance, they would be put out of communion. From Tertullian we should gather that a major responsibility lay upon the clergy for giving to those who undertook penance the support of Christian intercession. But beyond this, there is no sign of the clergy taking positive steps to foster and control Second Repentance, in any of the evidence cited, if we except the action of St John in Clement's legend.

We may therefore summarize the second century movement of thought with regard to the forgiveness of sins as follows. When the century opened, the rigorist tradition remained unmodified. The movement for its modification does not seem to have originated with the Church leaders but largely with the lay people. As the result of this movement, rigorism was relaxed during the second half of the century to this extent; that Christians with burdened consciences could have hope of being saved at the day of judgment, if the Church continued to own them as within the fellowship, while they accepted, and persevered in, a way of life much more austere and world-renouncing than the life that was required of them as the consequence of their baptism. Should the person who thus made Second Repentance fail to persevere to the end, in the life of penance, no renewal of repentance was open to him on the same terms. There seems to have been some feeling that no repentance could, in this life, be wholly unavailing, but the congregation could not hold out its hands to aid the backslider from Second Repentance. At the most, it could only admit him to a place with the hearers at the liturgical gathering. That must have meant that he was not wholly excluded from pastoral care, and it certainly cannot have cut him off from the sympathies and private prayers of Christians. However, for practical purposes there was one, and only one, Second Repentance in the fellowship of the Church. During the second Christian century the Roman Rule of Faith was in formation, with its third section dealing with the work of the Holy Spirit, which seems to lay its emphasis upon the redeemed community as the scene of that work. Part of this is expressed in the brief and enigmatic clause, 'the forgiveness of sins'. Nothing shows whether this work is believed to be tied to baptism or not, but it is clear that it is tied to the Holy Catholic Church, the communion of saints. Our Nicene creed acknowledges 'one baptism for the remission of sins'. It is accordingly likely that the older formula meant 'forgiveness of sins' to be associated with baptism in the Catholic Church. This would, at any rate, be the line of instruction to candidates for baptism. We could not expect Second Repentance and the forgiveness of sins after baptism to receive any place in the baptismal Rule of Faith.

CHAPTER FOUR

Progress by Penitence

C LEMENT OF ALEXANDRIA had the mind of a philosopher,
and integrated the Christian faith, as he received it in the
tradition of the Church and in Scripture, with an eclectic
philosophy of a dominantly Platonic cast. He was bound, therefore, to be drawn away from the rigorist tradition, rooted as it
was in eschatological expectations. For eschatology thinks of the
moment when the temporal order will yield to be merged into
the eternal order, while in Platonism the two orders exist over
against each other, in an unchanging relationship of distinction.
The eschatologist lives for the Day of the Lord to come, while
the Christian Platonist lives for the Lord to wean him from the
temporal and lead him into communion with the eternal. Clement
believed in a coming change in the relation of the temporal to the
eternal, but his thoughts about all that concerns man in this
present life were on the basis of an unchanging relationship.
Was he hellenizing Christianity? Or was the Christian message
being released from too exclusively Jewish an emphasis and so
made fit to do its work in an enduring catholic Church?

Clement thought as a Platonist, though as a loyally Christian
Platonist, when he thought about human sin and divine forgiveness. As Platonist, he saw the temporal order as being the world
of the imperfect, and sins as moral imperfections waiting to be
amended. As Christian, he saw the present age as the sphere in
which the Prince of evil has power to deceive souls to their hurt.

53

It was perhaps his loyalty to Christian tradition that led him to lay an exaggerated emphasis upon human freedom of choice with the result that he could recognize no strictly rational excuse for Christian sinning after baptism. On the other hand, he recognized that the passions provide a kindling, in every man's nature, for the devil to relight the fire quenched in baptism. So he embraced heartily the doctrine of Second Repentance for Christians, as it came to him commended by the authority of *The Shepherd of Hermas*. He seems to take that work at its face value as inspired Christian prophecy. He cites it, or draws upon it for his argument, in no less than twenty-one passages. It is from citation of *The Shepherd* that he starts the thirteenth lecture of his Second Book of *Stromateis*,[1] dealing with First and Second Repentance. He reasons that the whole fury of the devil is provoked by the sight of souls who receive in baptism that which he can never attain, plenary absolution. He says that it beseems God's mercy to grant to Christian victims of Satan's attack 'a repentance not to be repented of'. Clement justifies the once-for-all nature of Second Repentance by the consideration that if a further repentance were needed, it would only prove the insincerity of the Second Repentance. On the other hand, Clement had imbibed from his Greek literary education the maxim that it is of the nature of penitence to evoke sympathy. Therefore he believed that no repentance, if it really were repentance, could be in vain. So the problem of sin committed after baptism resolves itself, for Clement, into the simple question, 'Can the Christian sinner repent?' He sees the answer where the First Epistle of St John sees it, as depending upon the kind of sin that has been committed since baptism. Was it deliberate and deadly? Or was it involun-

[1] *Clement of Alexandria* (Ante-Nicene Christian Library XII) Vol. II, 1869, pp. 35–7.

tary and the fruit of surprise? The question whether there is need for Second Repentance would present no difficulty if it were possible to distinguish clearly between deliberate and undeliberate sinning. So Clement, in his *Stromateis*, expends much ingenuity, with the aid of allegorical interpretation of the Old Testament, in attempting to find the boundary between the two categories of sins. And when the attempt ends in failure, Clement draws the conclusion that we can never say, 'This Christian has so sinned that he cannot repent'. Therefore, as the legend of St John and the robber suggests, the privilege of Second Repentance can be denied to no one. On the other hand, Clement holds that the necessity of Second Repentance is matter for regret. He understands the saying 'In my Father's house are many mansions' as meaning that there are different degrees of glory among the saved. He thinks, therefore, that Christians who have had to resort to Second Repentance will find the bliss of salvation eternally mingled with regret for being severed in some way from those who kept the seal of their baptismal innocence intact. Thus Clement justifies 'Hermas' for not equating the fruits of Second Repentance to that plenary remission which is effected by baptism.

When we think of Clement's great conception of God the Word as Educator of human souls, and his postulate that all punishment must be corrective, it must surprise us that he did not conclude that souls were, under the leading of the Word, to make progress by a series of repentances. The fact that he did not do so, but halted firmly upon the ground that, for grave sins after baptism, there is only one repentance, testifies how loyal he was to Christian tradition. The step which Clement thus refrained from taking was, however, taken by his successor in the Christian Platonist school of Alexandria, the native Alexandrine,

Origen,[1] active from the second to the fifth decade of the third century. There can be no doubt that at that time the gap between ideal and actual in the Christian congregations was widening. It was this deterioration that caused Tertullian to leave the Catholic Church and seek the primitive purity of the faith in Montanism. Origen, however, stopped short of schism. A sharp critic of evils in the Church, he continued to acknowledge the authority of the Church. But to find the true life of Christians, he retreated into a conceptual inner Church composed of spiritual men, a *corps d'élite* within the Christian people, a company of true saints of Christ forming, as it were, the soul that kept the visible Body of Christ alive, in spite of its apparent regress from the Kingdom of God. Origen conceived himself to be the servant of the empirical Church, but his thinking and teaching was, in the main, directed towards that inner Church, the fellowship of spiritual men.

Now there is nothing that the spiritual man knows more surely than the subtle infiltration of temptation into the mind. Deplored and involuntary as are the sins into which even the most earnest servants of God are thus surprised, they yet form the proper subject of repentance. But such repentance is not necessarily, nor generally, that once-for-all Second Repentance recognized as such in the empirical Church. There is a repentance that is individual and spontaneous, like that of the Old Testament saints. For Origen believed that whatever is written in the Old Testament was prepared beforehand for the guidance of the spiritual Christian. Therefore if the saints of old repented and confessed their sins, as occasion arose, and were assured of divine forgiveness, so will it be with the spiritual Christian. But the people in the ordinary congregations did not think of the Old Testament in the same way as Origen. For them it was merely

[1] See C. Bigg, *The Christian Platonists of Alexandria*, 1913, pp. 260f.

the record of God's dealings with mankind in the past. And so, when they heard, from Leviticus, about the sacrifices for sins under the old law, they grumbled that, whereas the Lord's people in old times had had repeated sacrifices for sins, Christians have but one. For, they said, there is remission of sins in baptism and then no further provision for forgiveness. Origen makes the debating reply that those who know that Christ died for them ought not to resent a discipline more strict than that allotted to those who lacked such knowledge. But he follows that up by saying that there are, in fact, more ways of obtaining remission of sins under the New Covenant than under the Old. Christians, he asserts, have seven sacrifices for sins: the first is baptism, the second martyrdom, the third (argued from Luke 11.41) alms-giving, the fourth an act of forgiveness of others (such as is required of us in saying the Lord's Prayer), the fifth (based on James 5.20) by converting a sinner (who may be oneself), the sixth (inferred from Luke 7.47, the sinner who 'loved much', confirmed by I Peter 4.8, based on Prov. 10.12) an outpouring of love, and the seventh, ecclesiastical penance. This institution Origen assumes to be known to his readers. What form it now took will be considered in our next chapter.

In reciting these seven ways of seeking forgiveness, Origen has answered the complaint of the ordinary people, but only the spiritual were likely to take notice of his fourth, fifth and sixth 'sacrifices for sins'. So it is for the spiritual that Origen, in this *Second Homily on Leviticus*,[1] proceeds to unfold the allegorical meaning of the law of sacrifices for sins. The priest, he says, made the offering for himself and for those who provided the sacrifice. This shows that such sacrifices availed 'for involuntary sinners'. Wilful sinners are excluded from the benefit of such sacrifices,

[1] In Migne *PG*, 17. 17–20.

and this rule extends to four of the New Testament 'sacrifices'. In this allegory, Origen interprets the priest as representing our own sense of piety and religion. So, of the seven ways of sacrifice, three to six inclusive are for spiritual Christians and provide them with a way of progress by penitence on account of such sins as the ecclesiastical discipline passed over; anger, intemperance, lesser forms of dishonesty and untruthfulness, and the like. For such faults it was not appropriate to apply for public penance. And yet they are evils which require to be purged from the lives of Christians as a condition of their sanctification. To such an observer as Origen it was patent that they were being committed continually, even by the better among the members of the empirical Church. For such an evil Origen assumed that God must have provided a remedy, and, armed with the resources of allegorical interpretation of Scripture, he found it in the provision of spiritual sacrifices for sins.

At this point Origen cited James 5.16, 'Confess therefore your sins one to another, and pray one for another, that ye may be healed.' This again gives a practice designed for spiritual men. Such Christian penitents will turn to seek aid from the spiritual fellowship within their reach, in the person of a neighbour also a spiritual Christian. He need not be a priest by office in the empirical Church, to give the help of comradeship and counsel by which the penitent may come to the assurance of divine forgiveness. For since, in Origen's belief, every spiritual Christian exercises what is truly a priestly ministry in God's sight, any such brother may be a confessor to a spiritual man in his need. So Origen conceives a form of private confession.

This confession, while it has nothing to do with the public discipline of the empirical Church, is, so Origen says, a counsel for spiritual Christians, whereby, with the use of the appropriate 'sacrifices for sins' and their own repentance, they may turn their involuntary sins into the means of their sanctification. Origen does not deny that no Christian ought to sin at all after baptism, and he tells Celsus that 'on rare occasions some are to be found who have not sinned since their conversion' (*Contra Celsum*[1] III.69). These persons, he says, were not sinless before baptism, and it was only by their turning to the saving Word that they attained this sinlessness. Thus he represents post-baptismal sin-lessness as a moral miracle granted by God to the choicest of his human creatures. He says that it was seen more in the first days of the Church than recently. For those who are not sinless, all their sins whether involuntary or deliberate, must be purged in the appropriate manner. Spiritual Christians, whose sins are all involuntary, are purged and proceed to their perfection in the private way that has been described. More grievous sinners will require to be purged through the corporate discipline of the Church, a harder way which Origen describes, in reply to Celsus, in the words, 'Christians mourn as dead those who have been overcome by self-indulgence or outrageous sin, because they have died to God. They readmit them some time later, as though they had risen from the dead, provided that they show a real conversion; though their period of probation is longer than that which they had before they became Christians' (*Contra Celsum*[2] III.51). Thus Origen recognizes two forms of Christian repentance; a once-only repentance of grave or deliberate sins, and the other a repeated repentance of slight or involuntary sins.

In fact, Origen's thoughts sped far away beyond the ranks of Christians, whether spiritual or indifferent, so that he conceived the salvific will of God for all his creatures to be ultimately in-

---

[1] H. Chadwick, *op. cit.*, p. 175.
[2] *Op. cit.*, pp. 163f.

vincible. But in this universalist doctrine the Church refused to follow him. Nevertheless, so great was his influence upon the leaders of the Greek-speaking Church in the Eastern provinces in the following generation that the rigorist cause there was dead, and the very fact that it had existed, together with its *raison d'être*, the eschatological tension of the first age, was forgotten. In the Platonized Christianity which Greek Christendom owed so largely to Clement and Origen, the oft-repeated repentances of Christians were accepted, in as far as they were sincere, as a means of their spiritual progress. And this changed outlook on the forgiveness of the sins of Christians won its way into the Latin West as well, in spite of the taint of heresy that was, at the end of the fourth century, affixed to Origen's memory. With this changed outlook went two corollaries which are evident in germ in the thought of Clement and Origen. The first is that however difficult it may be to set the boundary between the two categories of sins, there are two such categories. They may be called deliberate and involuntary, or mortal and venial. Each has its appropriate remedy. The second corollary is that Christians can be divided into two classes: spiritual Christians, who live in godly fear of mortal sin, continually seeking sanctification by repentance of venial sins; and indifferent Christians who live in peril of grave lapses, and have hope of salvation only through the ministrations of the Church.

The establishment, in this way, of a recognition of two classes of Christian, came, in the fourth century, to receive visible representation in the distinction of a religious from a secular life within the Church. In fact, it was the practice of sanctification by penitence, as much as anything, that paved the way for the development of the former.

CHAPTER FIVE

A Discipline of 'Loosing'

THE power of the Church on earth to 'bind and loose' has sufficient scriptural grounding in Matt. 16.19 and 18.18, with John 20.23. Any exercise of this power must appertain to her pastoral function. It has appeared, in Chapter III, that down to AD 200 the bishops, as pastors, had exercised their function of loosing in the font, and their function of binding by withholding baptism or communion. But it was not long into the third century before the bishops began to combine the functions of binding and loosing, in exercising a pastoral control of the now established practice of *exomologesis*. This is hardly surprising. The discipline of excommunication had always carried within itself the possibility of its reversal. There was apostolic authority for the restoration of an offender who, when placed under discipline, submitted himself. How much more should the pastor wish to restore the Christian who voluntarily and publicly sought the aid of the Church, towards the 'loosing' of his burden of sin committed since baptism! As St John, in Clement's legendary tale, gave his oath to the robber that his Second Repentance should obtain for him remission, so it might seem to belong to the pastoral function of the bishops to give a like assurance, when the circumstances justified it, to Christian penitents of their flock. Nevertheless, when the bishops of Rome and of Carthage took the step of making it known, in the church, that they would exercise such discretion, each was answered by violent protests from within the church of his jurisdiction.

In the case of Rome, the protest came from the talented presbyter Hippolytus, who was in charge of a Roman congregation, which he proceeded to sever from communion with the Roman bishop, Callixtus. Unfortunately all our evidence comes from the pen of Hippolytus, who, in an anti-heretical work called *Philosophumena*,[1] proceeded to place Callixtus in his gallery of heretics. The two men had clashed, some time before, on a question of theology, while Zephyrinus, who died in AD 217, was Pope. Callixtus was his successor, and Pope for five years. The rancour which he excited in Hippolytus rendered that puritan quite unreasonable, and what he says about his *bête noire* is to be taken with ample salt. Nevertheless he can be so far believed, that Callixtus did what Zephyrinus had not done and made known his willingness to reconcile Christian penitents who submitted themselves to his pastoral authority. Thus we can fix upon the year AD 220 as approximately the time of the Roman introduction of episcopal control of Second Repentance. About the same time, Tertullian went into schism from the bishop and church of Carthage and exposed his reasons for so doing in a work entitled *On Modesty*.[2] Some have supposed it to be aimed at Callixtus, but it would more probably be directed against those from whom Tertullian had recently severed himself. In this case it will have been the bishop of Carthage whose declaration of willingness to restore penitents provoked the wrath of Tertullian. Perhaps the bishop specified certain secret sins with regard to which he was ready to exercise his pastoral responsibility. Unfortunately, in this case, one of the specified sins was fornication.

[1] I.e. *The Refutation of all heresies* (Ante-Nicene Christian Library VI) vol. I, 1868. See especially pp. 338–45.
[2] *On Purity* (Ancient Christian Writers 28), 1959.

It was this that roused Tertullian to extreme indignation. Tertullian makes the bishop say, 'Adultery and fornication'. But as he goes on straightway to argue that fornication is so far beyond the limit of what could be granted communicant repentance that, were it to be adultery, it would make no material difference, we must question whether adultery was specified. Presumably, in the eyes of the bishop, there would be a great difference between fornication and adultery. Under the circumstances of life in Carthage in the 220's, there was only too much probability that the secret burden on the conscience of a languishing Christian might be fornication. Tertullian, now a declared Montanist and puritan, shows us, in his work *On Modesty*, what his church would do for such a wretch. He would be exhorted to make a clean breast of it before the brethren. When he had done so, he would be commended to the righteous mercies of God. But he would be relentlessly cast forth from the communion of the Body of Christ on earth.

Tertullian does not spoil his case by denying to bishops all power of pastoral discipline, or the right to pardon where they have admonished. But in Ch. 7 he narrows down the exercise of this right to offences of comparative moral insignificance. In this he was certainly going beyond what was generally believed. A letter of Dionysius of Corinth,[1] written about AD 180, counsels the restoration of those who return from error of conduct or doctrine, without any proviso that such error must be slight. But the motive for Tertullian's exaggeration is clear enough. He wishes to take away from baptized persons who have subsequently committed certain sins the possibility of a Second Repentance within the communion of the Church. He could hardly have sustained such an attempt if the exercise by bishops of such a

[1] See Eusebius: *Hist. eccl.* 4.23.

'discipline of loosing' had not been something comparatively new.

Tertullian ends the book in question with a reference to the possibility of a renewal of persecution. He prophesies that, if this comes, the martyrs belonging to the church from which he is now in schism will be thronged, in their prisons, by remorseful lapsed Christians, begging them for their intercession with God. It might well be thought that the merit of the martyrs would prevail where no other earthly intercession could. But there was another reason why the martyrs might be sought in this way. In the exaltation of their hour of bearing witness for Christ, there was a hope that they might be inspired, like St John in Clement's legend, to swear to the penitents that their repentance would be rewarded with divine pardon.

This scene is only, at this stage, presented to the imagination. And Tertullian surveys it with angry contempt. But no doubt it was a prospect that was not absent from the minds of Catholic pastors. They would think of persecution falling upon poor creatures with sins such as fornication upon their consciences. They would think of them being arrested and, in their utter lack of moral courage, denying Christ, and even descending to give information against members of the Church. With such a prospect before his eyes, a bishop might well take any step that would put courage and confidence into the weaker brethren, while peace lasted, so that, when the shock of persecution came, it might find them in such solidarity with the Church that they would stand firm. So we have here evidence, from about the third decade of the third century, for a possible incentive for bishops to take the initiative with regard to Second Repentance.

Just because of rigorist opposition, bishops tended to increase the severity of the labours to be undertaken by the penitents, as a *satisfactio* offered to God. It must be emphasized that, at this date, the normal meaning of *satisfactio* was 'adequate apology'. But when the bishop became the judge of the adequacy of the *satisfactio*, it was natural that it should come to be viewed as *poena* (penalty).

A third protest against sacerdotal claims to restore Christian penitents who had fallen into grave offences occurs in Origen's book, *On Prayer*[1] (Ch. 28.10). This work was written at Caesarea in Palestine, shortly after Origen came thither from Alexandria, and so is to be dated about AD 235. The passage in question may be no more than an echo of the Western protests considered above. Origen does not even say that the offending pastors are bishops. In his eyes, the true priesthood under the New Testament is that exercised by spiritual Christians. There is, therefore, always a degree of uncertainty whether he is talking of those who hold office in the empirical Church or not. Bishops in that Church should be perfect priests, in the spiritual sense. But Origen knew of those who held the office but did not understand 'the laws of priesthood'. It is therefore most likely that he is referring to actual bishops when he says, 'There are some who, I know not how, have taken to themselves powers beyond the priestly dignity, perhaps because they are unversed in the craft of priesthood, and boast that they can forgive idolatries and remit fornications and adulteries, as though, through their prayer for those who have dared to do these things, the sin which is unto death is loosed'. The puritan in Origen is here visible, in his implication that the fornication of a Christian is a 'sin unto death', for which (following I John 5.16) a Christian must not intercede.

This expression of rigorism is, however, unique in the works of Origen. Many other passages of later date show that he re-

[1] Translated with notes by E. G. Jay, 1954. Also Ancient Christian Writers 19, 1954.

E

treated from the idea that nameable crimes could be specifically
excluded from the possibility of expiation through the Church.
He continued, however, to deny to Second Repentance the fruit
of a plenary absolution such as that conveyed by baptism. Its
only reward could be restoration to communicant life, with hope
of salvation at the Last Day. But it is abundantly clear, from
Origen's writings as a whole, that the passage cited above is no
evidence of opposition to the institution of Second Repentance,
as it existed in the empirical Church. He both acknowledged it,
and taught that sins grave enough to call for ecclesiastical penance could have that remedy but once, whereas involuntary sins
could have the oft-repeated aid of the appropriate 'sacrifices for
sins'. Origen also recommends for these sins, as we have seen,
confession to a spiritual brother. In *Homily II on Ps. 37* he men-
tions the possibiliy that this brother-confessor may counsel the
confessing of a particular sin publicly, in the congregation. But
to make such a confession would not be, in itself, the equivalent
of ecclesiastical penance, for, in ecclesiastical penance, the thing
that was made public in the congregation was not the nature of
the particular sin or sins, but only that they were such as to call
for the aid of the Church for their loosing. With regard to
ecclesiastical penance, Origen, who was always jealous of the
exercise of high spiritual functions by clergy who were not themselves spiritual men, so far qualifies his acceptance of episcopal
action as to declare, in his *Commentary on Matt.*, xii.14, that
a bishop bound in sin cannot loose sinners. This may give the
measure of significance of the somewhat petulant passage in the
work *On Prayer*, cited above. It is a last, but futile, voice of
protest against the completion of a movement whereby bishops,
throughout the Church, took pastoral control of the practice,
already established among the congregations, to which Tertullian

gave the name of *exomologesis*. The objective of this movement had therefore been consolidated, for more than fifteen years, when, in AD 249, the Decian persecution broke upon the Church.

Now was seen in fact, what Tertullian had foreseen in imagination, the recourse of the lapsed to the martyrs in prison; and we have abundant evidence of what followed, in the works of St Cyprian of Carthage and particularly in his treatise, *On the Lapsed*.[1] Cyprian had, but a short time previously, succeeded to the see of which a former holder was probably the man attacked by Tertullian in the work, *On Modesty*. But there appears to have been subsequently some degree of reconciliation, for Cyprian is authentically in a tradition that shows some of the characteristics that carried Tertullian into Montanism, and is recorded to have been a constant student of Tertullian's writings.

In the interval between the two men, the native population of Rome's African provinces, the country that now constitutes Algiers, Tunisia and Morocco, was being fast gathered into the Church. As a consequence, Christian Africa was becoming conscious of itself as such, by contrast with pagan Rome. So African Christianity took on a nationalist tinge. The constant holding of episcopal synods, in formal resemblance to the Roman senate, and that we can liken to a parliament of Christian headmen from all the African townships, became a special feature of the African Church. Therefore when the persecution of Decius was applied to Africa, its impact was upon a large, well-ordered and resistant body of Christians. And the success with which African Christianity sustained the shock was largely due to the assumption, by the clergy, of that pastoral discretion and authority that had roused the ire of Tertullian, thirty years before.

[1] In *St Cyprian* (Ancient Christian Writers 25), 1957 (Prof. Bévenot's notes are important for our subject).

Cyprian's work on *The Unity of the Church*[1] may be regarded as the first draft of a Western political theory of the Church. And it is one that assigns to the clergy a judicial function, or magistracy in spiritual things. The clergy, of course, always had had such a function, both in judging the fitness of candidates for baptism and in exercising the discipline of excommunication. But this juridical aspect of the priestly office was now, in Africa, brought very much to the fore by the effect of the Decian persecution. While an overall impression must be of the success with which the churches in Africa met the challenge, a still distressing number sought to save their liberty, or their property, by bowing to the decree requiring all citizens to placate the gods of Rome by acts of pagan worship. The length to which such infirm Christians had to go, to win the security they desired, varied from complete apostasy in the worst cases, to a skilful avoidance of the necessity of declaring themselves on the part of the more scrupulous. Then, over against the lapsed in every degree, were the Christians of heroic stature who incurred loss, imprisonment and finally death, in loyalty to their Christian faith. And the instinct of the lapsed, when they recoiled from their own disloyalty, was to rush to the prisons where the confessors were awaiting execution, to seek help and encouragement from these martyrs-designate, with a view to restoration to Christian communion. Some confessors luxuriated in the sense of spiritual power created by the common belief in their inspiration, without possessing the spiritual discretion to appreciate the real needs of the penitents applying for reconciliation. Thus by granting pardon these heroes of the hour merely covered up wounds which continued to fester.

So long as the persecution continued, the situation grew more

[1] In *Early Latin Theology* (Library of Christian Classics V), 1956, pp. 124–42. Cf. Ancient Christian Writers 25, above.

and more confused. But when it ceased, as it did after less than
two years, the confusion yielded to an exercise of spiritual magistracy on the part of the bishops in synodical agreement. The
situation with regard to the penitents' guilt which called for
episcopal discretion differed from that which was before their
predecessors in AD 220. Then the guilt of fornicators was secret,
and those who answered the bishop's call to Second Repentance
did so at the sole bidding of their consciences. The guilty in the
Decian persecution, on the other hand, were, for the most part,
not left to the promptings of their own consciences. Their guilt
was a matter of common knowledge, though there were some
whose guilt was only that of an inward and secret cowardice,
unknown to any but themselves. Nevertheless, all had sinned in a
way that lay outside the province of simple admonition or other
mild and private exercise of pastoral care. All must therefore be
urged to apply for ecclesiastical penance. But here the clergy met
with a peculiar difficulty. The depth of penitence of these lapsed
tended to vary inversely with the magnitude of their guilt.
Cyprian wrote his work *On the Lapsed* as part of a vigorous
campaign to bring the worst offenders to a sense of their desperate plight. To all the lapsed he offered the alternatives of
excommunication, and submission, in penance, to whatever
degree of humiliation and labour the Church, through her officers,
might impose upon them. So, if they clung to the hope of salvation, their first struggle had to be with themselves. They had to
reach the state of will to expiate their lapse by penance. Cyprian
represents them as not actually excommunicate at this stage, but
as naturally holding back, on their own initiative, from the
Eucharist, in recognition of their guilt. So their next step was to
make a full confession to the bishop, who then determined the
length of time that they must spend in making *satisfactio*.

Satisfactio meant, of course, making token, not full, amends, but nevertheless, such as were fitting in view of what they had done. So the bishop instructed them to fast, to pray, to dress as mourners, abstain from baths and pleasures of every kind, keep night vigils, sleep on the hard ground and, above all, to give alms. Then, in the congregation, the bishop publicly commended them to the prayers of the Church, whereupon they took the place allotted to penitents in the liturgical gathering. There is no evidence of any confession in the presence of the congregation, other than that silently made by the act of taking a place among the penitents. Cyprian seems to apply the title *exomologesis* to the whole series of acts of the penitent that were visible to the congregation, until the end of the assigned period. Then, *exomologesis* having been faithfully completed by the penitent, the bishop laid his hand upon him, for his reconciliation and restoration to the communion of the faithful. The aim of this imposition of a single hand seems to be the recalling of the Holy Spirit, repelled by grave sin. It was, in fact, Cyprian's criterion of *crimen mortale*, the sin that requires public penance, that there is evidence, in guilty fear and loss of faith, that the Holy Spirit has left his temple. But the Holy Spirit never deserts the Church: if the sinner can be held in the Church till reconciliation, he will return in the act of restoration. But it is only by a Catholic bishop, Cyprian teaches, that the Holy Spirit can be thus recalled. And this reconciliation or *pax* (peace) which the bishop gives at the completion of penance, is sacramental, in the sense of an *opus operatum*, a deed which has only to be done to carry with it the grace of heaven. And yet, even so, the *pax* remains conditional. If the penitent has gained it by deception, he will meet with Christ's final condemnation. In any case it does not restore the penitent to the same status as the faithful who have not sinned.

For though restored to communion, those who underwent Second Repentance remained for life under certain disabilities. In the same manner as the adequacy of his penitence had been the subject of pastoral examination while he was under penance, he remained thereafter under special pastoral care lest he should ever fall back again. On the other hand, however heinous the sin that brought him to penance, once the church had accepted him to *exomologesis*, he could live in hope that, at least on his death-bed, he might find reconciliation with the Church on earth, on the way to the final pardon of God.

Besides apostasy, and lapse under persecution, Cyprian seems to think of sexual licence, fraud and ecclesiastical revolt as making up the general range of sins calling for public penance. Tertullian, while Catholic, had had a wider list of grave sins, but when Montanist, and so regarding grave sin as irremissible, he narrowed the list, and this perhaps influenced Cyprian.

So thoroughly did Cyprian follow out the doctrine that the Catholic Church is the sole dwelling-place of the Holy Spirit, that he supposed that if a lapsed person afterwards underwent martyrdom, but without having been reconciled to the Church, he would be lost. He found the pardon granted by Catholic martyrs to the lapsed a more difficult case to argue. But it is clear that he would grant that their pardon had value only if, and when, it led to ecclesiastical reconciliation. To the theological argument, Cyprian added a practical consideration. Nothing but ecclesiastical penance would ensure the personal *operatio* of the penitent. Cyprian held that these costing works of repentance that he designates as *operatio* are owed, and must be paid. It is a weakness of his teaching that he does not relate the *operatio* of the penitent to the merits of Christ's death. This makes him largely responsible for the growth of the idea that *operatio* really means the payment of penalties fixed by a tariff relating them to the nature of the offence.

An aspect of the administration of *exomologesis*, in Africa of the mid-third century, is the extent to which it draws the clergy into responsibility for the success of Second Repentance. Once the penitent had been accepted to penance, it became almost as much the anxiety of the clergy as of the penitent that the undertaking should attain its due end. During the time of penance, the clergy must intercede with tears, 'offer sacrifice' for the penitent and join in making *satisfactio* with and for him. In them 'the Son of Man hath power in earth to forgive sins', and they must see that the exercise of their responsibility shall accord with Christ's heavenly judgment. The body of lay people in the congregation are implicated, through their clergy, in the struggle to save the wounded member under penance; for while there are penitents, all must grieve and all must pray.

There is no evidence that, at this stage, Christian penitence took any other ecclesiastical form than *exomologesis*. Many have argued that, in spite of this lack of evidence, there must have been also private penance. The pursuit of this argument has gone to prove that there is lack of evidence. But it has then been urged that the once-for-all character of Second Repentance would sentence the once reconciled, who sinned again, to lifelong excommunication. This, it is said, would have placed the assurance of forgiveness beyond the reach of moderate sinners. But we meet with much evidence, over several centuries, of exactly this difficulty being experienced and not overcome, so that it is clear that there cannot have existed the alternative of a private and repeatable penance. It is true that, for daily sins that are incurred after baptism and are not such as to call for *exomologesis*, Cyprian counsels *operatio*, particularly in the forms of fasting and giving of alms. But this is simply pastoral advice and forms a Western parallel to Origen's 'sacrifices for involuntary sins'. All our pictures of early Christian life would assure us that, as occasion arose, Christians would unburden their consciences to their clergy or their brethren, without compulsion, and receive spiritual comfort and guidance. But there is no positive ground for thinking that, in these early centuries, bishops ever laid penances upon Christians privately.

When Cyprian suffered martyrdom under Valerian, he had vindicated, for the Church in Africa, the principle of the spiritual magistracy of the clergy. His victory, it is true, was not unopposed. The persistence of rigorist feeling in the Church found its leader in Novatian, another Roman presbyter in the tradition of Hippolytus. But when he placed himself at the head of a schismatical communion, he carried the rigorist cause into the Novatianist sect, and the cause of rigorism died out within the Catholic Church.[1] So pastoral control spread and developed everywhere.

We have evidence of a special development taking place in North Asia Minor shortly after the death of Cyprian. In Pontus another mass conversion of the native people had been going forward, under the leadership of Gregory, bishop of Neo-Caesarea, a favourite pupil of Origen, and commonly known as St Gregory Thaumaturgus. Before there had been time for the population of the Pontic dales to be well established in the Christian way of life, the weakness of the Eastern empire, following the defeat and capture, by the Persians, of Valerian, permitted the Goths to pour down into Asia Minor. The Goths soon withdrew, but not before they had occasioned disorders of all sorts in the

[1] Lactantius thought that Satan inspired Novatianism so as to stop post-baptismal sinners escaping from his clutches.

young church in Pontus. We have a letter[1] of Gregory to a brother bishop, advising him upon the best way to restore Christian order. He ends by proposing progressive restoration of Christian penitents. He characterizes five stages in penance, beginning with the self-humiliation of the penitents before the Christian assembly, much as Tertullian describes it in his work *On Penitence*. But it is expressly said that some offenders, those showing the desire to put right what they had done wrong, should be excused the first two stages on the road to restoration. Here again we have the effect of circumstances in moulding the development of the episcopal control of Second Repentance. In this case it is through the temporary weakness of the secular authority giving scope to the exercise of spiritual magistracy by the Christian clergy. With this fact we see combined the effect of mass conversion, inevitably followed by a fall in the standards of catechumenate. The baptized were not, in consequence, secure in their sense of conduct consistent with Christian faith and with the holiness of the Church. Therefore the clergy were fain to turn the necessity of penance into a more severe and exemplary recapitulation of catechumenate. Thus the third century scene closes with Christian pastorate finding one of its most exacting tasks in the care of the serious casualties, as regards the Christian life, among the flock under its charge. Morever, the handling of these 'casualties' was now recognized to be a special exercise of the power of the Church to bind and loose.

[1] In *Fathers of the Third Century* (Ante-Nicene Fathers VI), 1886, pp. 18–20

he asks, 'that the serpent has so lasting a poison, and Christ no remedy?' This was an apt way of stating his case, for the Constantinian revolution had created a strong impression in the minds of Christians that the progressive defeat of paganism must be a staggering blow to the Satanic powers. No idea could have had a more relaxing effect than this upon the moral tension in Christian life. On the other hand, it was an idea that favoured the claim of ecclesiastical penance to serve the completion of Christ's victory. So Pacian extols the use, by the Catholic Church, of such penance. He had to be careful, when arguing with a Novatian, how he applied to the baptized promises addressed in Scripture to the unbaptized, of the forgiveness of their past sins. Nevertheless we can read between the lines, in his letter, that the people who heard exhortation to penitence read from the Old Testament prophets, continued, after they had ceased to be catechumens, to take these exhortations as addressed to themselves. As a consequence, they were losing any sense of the enormity of post-baptismal sin as such. But those who felt the need of ecclesiastical penance still had to accept it as unrepeatable. Nevertheless, Pacian says that Catholics frequently undertake penance for sins that are not *peccata talia*, sins of a gravity commensurate with such a step. And in spite of the grave consequences that might follow from using, without necessity, a means to assurance of forgiveness that cannot be repeated, Pacian apparently regards the course he has described as commendable. But it is probable that those who took this course did so with the intention of adopting a stricter and more religious way of life. Accordingly, the danger that, after doing penance, they would fall into such backsliding as to incur lifelong excommunication, might not be so serious. It would rather be those who were driven to penance by their commission of really grave sins who would most need subsequent protection from the risk of backsliding. Such persons were a heavy responsibility to the clergy. Sometimes they were taken to live in the church buildings, as lay servants of the church. But as the monastic movement spread in the West, a happier expedient was to commend such persons to the care of a monastic house, in whose ordered and ascetic life they would find it possible to persevere in their penitential behaviour. Such reconciled penitents, living in monasteries, came to be called *conversi*, a title which, in course of time, came to be applied to all lay brethren and sisters living in religious communities. Another consequence of the spread of monasticism was that the kind of person who, in Pacian's day, would seek penance for sins that were not *peccata talia*, would, in later times, seek the religious life, directly and under life vows. The point of Pacian's reference to these voluntary seekers of penance is that they illustrate the use of ecclesiastical penance to forward, and not to endanger, the holiness of the Church. Pacian's antagonist replies that, in the ecclesiastical remission of post-baptismal sins, fallible men may involve the Name of God in the condoning of evil. Pacian answers that justice will always triumph at the Last Day, and the normal use of the power of the keys in the Catholic Church is no misuse. It is exercised with divine approval and authority, and the ministry of the Church, cooperating with the penitence of those who come to Second Repentance, obtains for them their forgiveness by God. Thus we see that, within fourth-century Catholicism, the notion of the Church as 'an ark to save the perishing' was gaining over the notion of the 'congregation of saints'. Meanwhile society outside the Church recognized that in the forefront of the advantages for which men embraced the Christian faith was the forgiveness of sins. And while there were those who asked derisively, 'How can deeds that have been done, be undone by recitation of words?', everyone regarded the claim of the Church to release men from the guilt of sins as her most characteristic and fundamental claim. Thus the pagan historian Zosimus, while sneering at the asserted Christian promise to Constantine that the Church could show him a way to perfect cleansing from those crimes upon which Zosimus had been glad to dwell, saw in it the explanation of Constantine's espousal of the Christian cause. On the other hand we see Eusebius including nothing in his *Life of Constantine* inconsistent with perfect sanctity on the part of the deceased emperor, because Constantine's deathbed baptism had wiped from the tablets of godly memory all record of his misdeeds. Under such circumstances, redemption from sin through Christianity became an element of popular thought. The mood of mockery, associated with it for a time, subsided, and the power of the Church to remit sins came, instead, to be regarded as a boon for the sake of which any man might, sooner or later, have recourse to her. But once popular thought had, in this way, begun to busy itself with the subject, theologians might struggle in vain to resist the effects within the congregations. A great part of the baptized regarded their assurance of forgiveness and their hope of final salvation, as implicit in their possession of Catholic communion. Nevertheless, not everything in Christendom at this time was making for the relaxing of moral tension in the Church. A movement in the opposite direction had begun before the end of the third century, by those who embraced the ascetic ideal, and set out to live the life of 'spiritual athletes'. In the first stage, these seem to have been men and women living among the congregation, but withdrawn in every way possible from secular business. The similarity of such a state of life to that required of a person reconciled after penance is obvious. But the third-century ascetics, so far from being persons who had needed Second Repentance, appear as being heroes of faith in the eyes of the ordinary congregation. Nevertheless, it was not so much ambition to excel, as fear of being conformed to the world, that seems to have been their motive.

The famous St Antony[1] was an ascetic of this kind, who was so impressed with the sternness of the spiritual war that he withdrew from the haunts of men into the Egyptian desert, to devote himself wholly to the quest of holiness. From this start is traced the rise of Christian monachism. A monastic movement quickly spread in Egypt, and from Egypt to Syria, Palestine, and Asia Minor. If a kind of spiritual ambition is unhappily in evidence in the records of early monasticism, at least the Origenist monks of Egypt followed Origen's counsel of sanctification by repentance of involuntary sins. It was, indeed, of vital importance to the ascetic life that it should be a penitent life, since otherwise it could not fail to lead to spiritual pride. But in spite of the dangers and weaknesses that beset the monastic movement, it appears, in the fourth century, as the chief Christian glory of the age. At the same time, the fact that so much Christian asceticism was thus diverted outside the life of the congregations prevented it from leading to general revival and reform. In fact it led to an acquiescence, on the part of the Church as a whole, in a double standard of Christian life, according to which the ordinary Church laity lived very much conformed to the world and left world-renunciation to monks. But there survived still, at the end of the fourth century, some following of an ascetic life within the secular congregations. In the Roman church Pelagius lived a protagonist of this ideal. He tried to make it the serious aim of every Christian, from the moment of his baptism, to live sinless. In this

[1] See *Athanasius: The Life of St Antony* (Ancient Christian Writers 10), 1950.

attempt, he found himself frustrated by what seemed to him a kind of moral defeatism among Christians, and learned that this mood was drawing encouragement from theologians.

In these circumstances, Pelagius insisted upon the truth which seemed to him all-important, namely that, while every man has free will, wherewith he can choose to serve God, Christians have many things to help them to make that choice consistently. So he made all his appeal to the right use of free will. Unfortunately for him, the opposition which he felt was based upon theological thought much more profound and subtle than his own. For the master-mind leading it was the mind of Augustine of Hippo, and it had now gained the solid adhesion of the African church. Then the sack of Rome by Alaric in AD 410 enhanced the importance of the African provinces to the Western empire, so that the African church felt strong enough to attack as heretical the over-simplified teaching of Pelagius, together with his supporters in Rome and Italy. When the Africans, in AD 418, secured the support of Pope Zosimus, the Western emperor gave their cause the support of the secular arm. Thus the last attempt to revive a rigorist outlook within Western catholicism was forcibly suppressed.

It was, however, only the growing weakness of the Western empire that made it so ready to lend the secular sword to the enforcing of ecclesiastical sentences, in return for moral and political support from the hierarchy. To this weakness of the state was now due a change in the administration of ecclesisatical penance. This transpires from one of Augustine's *Replies to diverse questions*.[1] It had been traditional for the penitent, at the end of *exomologesis*, and before receiving restoration, to make an explicit, if not detailed, confession. This custom was now given

[1] In Migne *PL*, 40.11–100.

up, and Augustine alleges, in explanation, that penitents might be in peril from the imperial police if their confession were disclosed. For the state, incapable of the consistent enforcement of law, resorted to the exemplary punishment of those offenders upon whom it was able to lay its hands. This was, at any rate, a plausible reason for the abandonment of a tradition and the substitution of secrecy with regard to the sins being expiated by ecclesiastical penance. We learn also, from the same source, that the falling off in the standards of Christian initiation was reflected in scandalous sins committed by baptized persons, without there being in them a degree of deliberate wickedness commensurate with the scandal. This was a further reason why the clergy, who first received the confession of the penitent in private, should not require a like disclosure in public. Thus, since the fear of civil punishment or of social scandal would keep sinners back from the desperate and only means of their salvation, the bishops held out assurance that there should be secrecy concerning the offences for which penance was being undergone. But this meant that a heavier responsibility than ever fell upon the bishops themselves, in assessing the nature and severity of the penance appropriate to the offence thus secretly confessed. It was not until long after Augustine made these *Replies* that we meet with explicit reference to the seal of the confessional, but in them we have the principle of the 'seal' acknowledged.

The decay of the Western empire continued, and bishops often found themselves the only effective arbiters, in the midst of a nominally Christian population, of social and moral righteousness. The reparations for transgression of the moral law and of social justice, which they directed, had now to fulfil the function formerly fulfilled by legal sanctions. Becoming thus administrators of an ecclesiastical law, the bishops were driven to turn legis-

F

lators. So we find a succession of episcopal synods of the fifth to the seventh centuries engaged upon the task of bringing uniformity to the administration of ecclesiastical penance. This was done by the passing of penitential canons, determining the length and nature of the penance to be demanded everywhere in respect to this or that offence. The practical necessity of proceeding on these lines is obvious. But such canons could take no cognizance of the state of conscience of the penitent, in earlier days the matter of first consideration in the administration of Second Repentance. They could only measure the satisfaction due by the enormity of the civil or moral *crimen* (crime) involved. If, as a result, a thinly Christianized legalism established itself, at least the people, conditioned as they were by the increasing barbarism of most Western lands, could, in this way if no other, be made to grasp, as it were by rule of thumb, the manner of the Christian life.

The point at which Christian values were most endangered lay in the notion, which the people readily entertained, that the giving to God of *satisfactio*, in the form of penances performed, was the obtaining of pardon at a price. The readiest expedient for meeting this danger was to mitigate the penance until the penitent could not but regard it as merciful. A theoretical justification, even for progressive mitigation of penances, was found in the doctrine of a corporate treasury of merit, inherited by the Church militant, and accumulated through the heroic virtues of the ever-growing company of saints in glory. The principle of the gratuity of divine forgiveness was thus partially restored to recognition. But the sense of the obligations involved in baptism continued to decline.

Another kind of mitigation in the undertaking of public penance was made from at least the seventh century. In the fifth century, on the testimony of Hilary of Arles, the penitent began his penance on the next Sunday after his application had been allowed. But at some time later it became the custom to postpone the entry on public penance until the following Lent began, at which time all the persons making Second Repentance began it together. The ordeal of undertaking penance was thus considerably reduced. But by this time, the discipline of public penance, as an effective part of ecclesiastical pastorate, was entering upon its last decline. The chief reasons for this decline were, of course, the diminishing moral tension in Christian life and the weakened cohesion of Christian congregations. These things carried with them increased difficulty in the protection of those who had done public penance, otherwise than by their 'incarceration' in a monastery. But the fact is that Western Christendom had, in the course of the fifth century, undergone a profound change of outlook on the subject of the sins of Christians, which, while it had no obvious and direct bearing on the institution of public penance, further modified the feeling of churchmen towards the gravity of post-baptismal sin. This change resulted from the teaching of Augustine on original sin. And it is to this subject that we must now pass.

CHAPTER SEVEN

Sin Original as well as Actual

THE belief that men are born with a nature in disorder, and with a bias towards vice, is well in evidence in the Old Testament. So also is a sense of human solidarity, even to the extent of involving children not only in the evil nature but also in the guilt of their ancestors. In St Paul's Epistle to the Romans, this solidarity in evil is connected with a primal sin committed by the first parents of the human race. These ideas, of an evil bias in every man's disposition and of human solidarity in evil, passed into the doctrinal heritage of the Church. But for three centuries they remained undeveloped. Christian theologians, reacting against the fatalism so prevalent in Eastern thought and the dualism that regarded matter as the source of evil, threw all emphasis upon the free will of every individual, assisted by a divine Providence regardful of man and his spiritual liberty. In consequence, Christian piety had a very moralistic colour, and so continued till the end of the fourth century. So much was this the case that, when Pelagius taught in a way that laid such stress upon the freedom of the will, he could not be accused of conscious innovation.

The outlook of the Eastern Church was, even more than that of the West, dominated by this emphasis on free-will. This was, in part a result of reaction against the teaching of Origen. Origen speculated that souls entered the world at birth guilty of pre-natal sin. But this sin, he taught, was their own individual sin and in no way depended upon the sin of Adam. When Origen left Alexandria, where he had known only the baptism of adult converts, and settled at Caesarea in Palestine, he met there, for the first time, the administration of baptism to the infant children of Christian parents. The baptismal liturgy, when infants were baptized, did not differ from that in use for adults. It was baptism for the remission of sins, a fact that seemed favourable to Origen's theory of pre-natal sin. But that theory rested in turn upon a Platonic doctrine of the pre-existence of souls which, in the form that Origen gave to it, was rejected by the Church. The result was that Eastern theologians had a reason for not questioning that infants are innocent at birth.

The custom of baptizing infants spread through Christendom. By the later years of the fourth century, the Church was everywhere accustomed to receiving in baptism the infant children of the baptized, especially if they were in danger of dying. To the men of that age the custom appeared of immemorial antiquity. No one could say that it had not been followed from the very first days. New Testament references to the baptism of households were, in fact, taken to prove that it had so been followed. Augustine was able to say, therefore, without fear of contradiction, that the Church had ever baptized infants for the remission of sins.

Against him, the Pelagians argued that, as it is inconceivable that every infant has committed some sin before baptism, the benefits that are sought for them in that sacrament must be benefits other than the remission of sins. The object of infant baptism, they said, was to give to these children the benefits of membership of Christ's Church. Augustine denied their premiss and said that since infants *are* baptized for the remission of sins, they are no sooner born than they are in need of forgiveness. They must all therefore, enter the world in a state of soul displeasing to God. Challenged to say how this could be, Augustine cited Rom. 5.12, in a Latin version that is not exact in rendering the original Greek. It made Paul say that every man sinned 'in Adam'. In the generation before that of Augustine, a Latin commentator on this passage, to whom it is usual to assign the name *Ambrosiaster*, had interpreted the verse more justifiably by saying that Adam sins in every man's person. This implies that Adam does not sin in any man's person, until that person sins. Pelagius, not unreasonably, followed this interpretation. But it was Augustine's interpretation of the verse that received general acceptance from Western churchmen. An infant, they supposed, was brought to baptism because he had sinned in Adam's person. Thus, although the infant did not, as a person, pre-exist, he was guilty of sin that was, in relation to him, pre-natal. To this pre-natal sin, on account of which every infant needs baptismal remission, Augustine applied the name of 'original sin'. Every infant, in course of time, adds to this original sin actual sins, for which he is directly and alone responsible. Now sins cannot be remitted by anticipation. If a person, when baptized, had already committed actual sins, they would be covered by the plenary remission effected in baptism. But when baptism was administered before there had been actual sin, then it released from original sin only. So, if a baptized infant died before commission of actual sin, his entry into the kingdom of heaven was assured.

It was the converse to this proposition that both caused Augustine agonies of thought, and was wholly unacceptable to the Pelagians, namely, that an infant dying unbaptized passed into the endless company of devils in hell. Following Ambrosiaster, Pelagius tried to establish a middle way, between damnation for all the unbaptized and the automatic salvation of all who died in infancy. This was that the souls of infants who died unbaptized would have eternal life, not indeed in the kingdom of heaven, but in some limbo, in which existence is an unmistakable good and not, like eternity in hell, an unimaginable evil. But Augustine, and afterwards the Western Church, rejected this solution. It was the conviction that sacraments must be necessary that made Pope Innocent prompt to condemn the Pelagian proposition. Neither he nor Pope Zosimus required Christians to hold the Augustinian doctrine of original sin. But the Council of Carthage, in AD 418, in its third canon, excluded the possibility of a fate other than hell for any who died unbaptized. Augustine's final teaching was that not all men, but only those brought to God by Christ, are saved; though these are representative of the whole race, and, in that sense, God is said to will the salvation of all men. In the course of a long literary activity, Augustine defeated every attempt to establish an alternative to his doctrine; that is to say, the doctrine of a race lost in sin, except in so far as a pure grace of God, exercised in Christ, delivered any soul from the company of devils, into God's eternal kingdom.

He was, however, very hard pushed by the Pelagian leader, Julian of Eclanum, onto the horns of a dilemma. One horn was to make the Creator responsible for the evil in his creatures upon whom he pours forth his wrath and condemnation. The other horn was to grant to evil and to the evil spirits, a substantial existence over against God. This was the Manichaean heresy, of which Julian suspected Augustine. To avoid this dilemma, Augustine asserted that all evil done by men or devils is the unsubstantial fruit of their creaturely wills. On the other hand, he saw in all evils suffered by men the manifestation of the righteous wrath of God against sin. To maintain this thesis he had to take his stand upon the ideal perfection of the original creaturehood of man and of the universe. This means that wherever an Augustinian doctrine of salvation is coupled with insistence upon the literal infallibility of Scripture, as in Roman Catholicism to-day, the historicity of man's original perfection becomes an article of faith. Only in modern times have there appeared strong reasons for doubting it.

From this point, therefore, we have to consider what difference the over-all triumph of Augustinianism in the fifth century made to Christian belief regarding the forgiveness of sins. The first thing is that it sets the whole subject of sin in a new perspective. In a large number of places, Augustine, by appealing to passages in earlier Christian writers, strives to demonstrate that his doctrine of original sin is no innovation. But, in passage after passage, it proves to be the case that Augustine's doctrine coincided not with what the theologian in question said, but only with Augustine's logical deduction from what the author said. Thus Augustine could rightly assert that his doctrine was implicit in the past teaching of the Church. But it remains that the over-all result of his teaching was to set the subject of human sin in a new aspect.

In the generations that preceded Augustine, Christian thought had been preoccupied almost exclusively with actual sins. Fearing to discourage effort, earlier teachers turned a blind eye upon man's powerlessness to make himself good, while Augustine saw clearly that only God can make man good. Therefore, at whatever stage in a man's life God's favour is known, as much when moving him to penance as when moving him to first conversion, forgiveness is assured to that person in and through the Church. For trust in the Catholic Church was fundamental to all Augustine's thinking, as was trust in the means of grace ordained by God to be ministered by the Church. And so, although his outlook was so different from that of the earlier teachers in whose hands the institution of ecclesiastical penance had grown up, Augustine accepted that institution as the means of the same undeserved grace and favour of God towards his elect as had formerly been bestowed upon them in their baptismal cleansing. Those who came after Augustine were, for the most part, far from entering fully into his outlook.

Actual sins were, however, seen by the post-Augustinian Church as incidents in the foreground of a scene dominated by the eternal purposes of God. Wherever the action of God is seen in the world of space and time, as in the Incarnation, the Church and the Sacraments, there, in the midst of this world's vanities, the significant and eternal is present and actual. And in as far as the Augustinian vision of God-in-action was a new vision, it spread a new kind of piety among Christians; a piety which, in comparison with that of a Pelagius, was humbler and more effortless. It was a piety to the appeal of which the Church of that age responded, where it failed to respond to the stimulus of Pelagianism. And in it the Platonic antithesis of the temporal and the eternal became domiciled in Christianity, in the form of an antithesis of nature and grace.

Augustine did not take baptism for a miracle in the world of nature. The will of the baptized was, he said, set free by a grace given in baptism to will good, but the natural bias to evil that accompanied the guilt of original sin remained. And therefore, grace notwithstanding, there cannot fail to be in every baptized person at least slight or involuntary sins, for which forgiveness must be sought day by day. Augustine relies on I John 1.8, to refute a claim to actual sinlessness on behalf of this or that human creature. But while he uses the word *peccata* (sins) for those transgressions which strew the lives of the elect on their way to eternal salvation, he uses the word *crimina* (grave sins) for those lapses which we rightly fear may mean our fall from grace, and the earning of damnation. He teaches his catechumens that they will commit *peccata* daily, for which they are to seek God's forgiveness directly, by the same New Testament means that Origen taught. And he tells them that the people whom they see doing penance in church have committed *crimina*, 'either adulteries or other heinous crimes'. But he hints at no dividing line between the two orders of sins. It is the prerogative of pastors to discriminate, and the people are not to think that they can judge of it for themselves, when the matter is at all in doubt. Augustine, in his *Enchiridion*[1] (64), says that, in the Rule of Faith, we profess belief in the Holy Catholic Church before we profess belief in the remission of sins. This shows, he says, that remission of sins takes place in the Church. So the life of the Church is guaranteed, not by its static purity, but by the continual forgiveness granted to her sinning members. We are reminded of a vision of Hermas (3.11–13), in which he sees the Church as an aged lady, rejuvenated whenever post-baptismal sinners respond to the call of the angel of penance. And that shows how far Augustinian piety is from being without precedent in Christian tradition. At the same time, by giving baptism its unique function in the remission of original sin and by then showing that we 'remain sons of men after we have been made sons of God', Augustine makes more clear the need for a Second Repentance, in the Church, to follow baptism. He did much, also, to exalt Second Repentance to sacramental status, by insisting that it could bring remission of post-baptismal sins only if performed within the Catholic Church. The Synod of Arles, in AD 314 had established the doctrine that

[1] In *Augustine: Confessions and Enchiridion* (Library of Christian Classics VII), 1955, pp. 337–412.

any baptism by water in the sacred Name of the Trinity gives baptismal remission, effective, at least, from the moment that the person so baptized is within the Catholic communion. But, said Augustine, the only post-baptismal sinner who can have his sins remitted is a Catholic, who is ready to make *satisfactio* (in the sense of due and loyal apology) to the Church for injury done to her sanctity and honour. And, he added, the remission of sins carries with it the remission of pains hereafter, for which mercy the pains of penance are but fitting acknowledgement.

But if public penance could be effective only within the Catholic Church, so, according to Augustine, was the daily remission of lesser sins. In speaking of this, he indicates that people were too ready to take a legalistic attitude and to think that remission of sins by almsgiving was the purchase of licence to sin again. Also they were apt to forget that the saying of the Lord's Prayer is only effective for forgiveness if the declaration of forgiving our debtors is sincere. A real way of 'converting a sinner', Augustine says, is to awake to the misery of one's own spiritual condition. It is fundamental, with Augustine, that forgiveness follows conversion, and every conversion is the pure and mysterious work of God's grace. So, on the one hand, the influence of Augustine in the Western Church favoured the concept of Christian religion as a seeking of God's glory, and, on the other, the defeat of the Pelagians was a set-back to Christian moralism. And such it was particularly felt to be by the young monastic communities of South Gaul. These owed their development to an exile from Egypt, the Origenist-trained John Cassian. In a book of imagined interviews with famous Egyptian leaders of the monastic life, Cassian taught Origen's way of sanctification by penitence. In one of these (*Collatio* 20)[1], the question asked is 'How can a

[1] Nicene and Post-Nicene Fathers XI, 1894, pp. 496–502.

Christian know that he is forgiven?' In general, the answer is
that when the sin in question is no longer repeated, and the
desire to commit it passes from the heart, the penitent can know
that he has received the forgiveness he sought. But when Cassian
cites, in this discussion, Acts 3.19 and Matt. 3.2, both addressed
to the unbaptized, to prove that repenting brings remission, it is
clear that, at least as regards lesser sins, the notion that baptism
makes any fundamental difference to the question of forgiveness, is passing out of mind. If the expected sinlessness of Christians after baptism, as it appears in the writers of an earlier age,
is not forgotten, it is now interpreted as freedom from what
Augustine includes under *crimina*.

The Gallican monasticism that developed under the influence
of Cassian was moralistic and tended to reproduce the Eastern
emphasis upon the freedom of the human will. Augustine's
relentless logic reduced to nothing man's power of willing good,
unless revived by an act of divine grace. This doctrine was felt
by many to challenge the monastic tradition and to make irra-
tional the practice of prayer and intercession, and the moral
discipline that was, throughout the Church, exercised by pastors.
A reaction against Augustinianism accordingly began, led by the
Gallican monasteries. Their thinkers tried to show that human
free-will cooperates with divine grace. And this attempt went on
for more than a generation, under the name of Semi-Pelagianism.
Both Semi-Pelagianism and Augustinianism remained beyond
the horizon of the theology of the Eastern Church, where there
has since been neither counterblast to Augustinianism nor any
development of thought on the subject of sin and forgiveness
comparable to that which has taken place in the West. From this
point onwards, therefore, we shall pursue the history of the doctrine of the forgiveness of sins only as it developed in the lands

of Western Europe; that is to say, in a Catholicism that, for many centuries, accepted the supremacy of the Roman see.

In the sixth century, with the activity of Caesarius, bishop of Arles, and with the Second Synod of Orange in AD 529, the strife between Augustinianism and Semi-Pelagianism is seen to die down in an atmosphere of compromise. The flagrant disorder within a nominal Christendom made the Augustinian doctrine of the weakened will for good in man, and of the necessity of grace for every good work, more acceptable. In the writings of Caesarius we seem to see a concentration of pastoral interest upon the devout minority in the Church, as upon those in whom saving grace is more probable. A particular way of seeking the glory of God is thus conceived to be the penitence of the devout for involuntary sins. For such persons, if they have upon their conscience a great total of lesser sins, Caesarius recommends ecclesiastical penance, partly on the ground that the price of such sins must otherwise be paid in purgatory. Those who, in answer to this counsel, came forward at the beginning of the penitential season to take the hair shirt received a laying-on-of-hands to bless their penance. And although they were thereafter liturgically put forth from the company of the faithful, they reappear at every solemn Mass. In fact, the chief part of their *operatio* appears to consist of assiduous attendance at church.[1] But such fruits of the excellent pastorate of Caesarius only show up the general decline of *exomologesis*. The troubled in conscience held back from communion, until they thought themselves to be dying. Then they applied for penance, and died in the hair-shirt. A much-publicized letter of Pope Siricius to a Spanish bishop precluded those who had made Second Repentance from marital

[1] The last form of public penance to survive was that of prescribed pilgrimage.

relations and the wearing of arms, for life.[1] Therefore no one would willingly apply for penance until they had no more to hope from life in the world.

For an adequate account of the difficulties which pastors encountered, during the fifth to seventh centuries, in trying to make public penance continue to serve the cause of the salvation of souls, the reader may turn to Dr R. C. Mortimer's *Origins of Private Penance* (1939). The fact that, century after century, no one thought it possible to question or alter the once-only character of the rite of public penance, or to modify its application in the case of less outrageous sins, gives us the strongest ground for presuming that the tradition of the Church from primitive days was one of expectation that Christians would live a life, after their baptism, conceived as in some sense sinless.

[1] In Migne *PL* 13.1137 (ch. 5).

CHAPTER EIGHT

Penance a Sacrament

THE Europe of which the ecclesiastical centre was the Roman see had an extreme Western fringe of Celtic peoples, whose Christianity was strangely detached from that of the continent. The Celts of Ireland remained mostly unevangelized until the middle-fifth century, although those of Great Britain were largely Christian, and in close touch with the Church in Gaul. But in AD 413 the British lost the protection of the Romans, and before long an inflow of Angles, Jutes and Saxons interposed a wall of heathendom between Christian Europe and the British Celts, now driven West into Cornwall, Wales and the Highlands of Scotland. At the same time, great numbers of fugitive Celts poured into Armorica (North-West France), which thenceforth became Brittany, a Britain beyond the sea. By this time the Irish had received an apostle in the person of St Patrick, a Briton from somewhere near the Bristol Channel. And though he took to them a Latin and Roman Christianity, the Irish Church soon appears in religious solidarity with other Celtic Christians. From the sixth century, Celtic Christianity appears as a detached limb of Western Christendom. Much of the individuality of the Celtic churches is to be explained as the fruit of conservatism on the part of a cut-off portion of the Church. Some of it was a legacy from the fugitive days, when the Celts were flying before the Germanic invaders. For, in that flight, the maintenance of Church life was only possible, we may suppose, by means of a clergy detached from all worldly possessions, and carrying religion to their people, as it were, in their bare hands. When Anglo-Saxons ceased to spread westward, and the flight of the Britons ended with settlement in their remaining territory, there was left a Celtic Christianity with the ministry and sacraments of the catholic Church. But the Celtic ministry was not based upon cathedral cities and territorial dioceses. It was based on monastic settlements containing many monks in Holy Orders, including some possessed of episcopal consecration. Celtic monachism reproduced the most primitive stage of the monastic movement as it arose in Egypt. The fugitive days of the Celts seem to have left their mark on Celtic monachism, in the form of a conviction that the monk should be a wanderer for God upon the earth. Ministry to the more recently Christianized was maintained by monks who went forth from their monasteries. And in the seventh and eighth centuries numerous Celtic monks went as missionaries to continental lands, and brought a breath of primitive zeal back to Latin Christendom.

There is no reason to doubt that, while Britain was within the Roman empire, the institution of public penance was as well known in the church of these islands as in Gaul. A number of ideas connected with *exomologesis* can be traced in later Celtic Christianity, but not the institution itself. This is made sure by the statement of Theodore of Tarsus, Archbishop of Canterbury in the seventh century, that public penance, as it went on at Rome at that period, was unknown in these islands.

The homilies and exhortations that did duty for monastic rules among the Celts reproduce faithfully the penitential tone of Egyptian monachism, as pictured in the writings of Cassian. Celtic monks made every incident of the monastic quest of vir-

tue into a work of penitence. In particular, the traditional confession of involuntary sins by one monk to another could be
made, in a Celtic monastery, to a bishop or priest. It seems to be
a filling of the gap left by the loss of *exomologesis* that moved
Celtic monks to ask of their confessor a penance. The sins thus
privately confessed were not always *crimina*, and the motive for
seeking penance was the desire to do the utmost to attain true
penitence and the assurance of divine forgiveness. The whole
transaction was voluntary and private to the two participants,
and the penitent was not excommunicate. It was like the 'pious
penance' counselled by Caesarius of Arles and like the confession
to a 'spiritual brother' taught by Origen. And it owed something
to the austere and self-afflicting spirit of the Celtic monks. But
the result was a new and distinct institution, the institution of
private penance, under the direction and ministration of a bishop
or priest who, as pastor gave counsel, as judge assigned penance,
and as holding the authority of the Church to bind and loose,
restored the penitent to his life as a Christian. The confession
was heard in a house, and afterwards both parties went to the
church building to pray; the confessor often fasted with the
penitent.

Starting thus among the Celtic monks, this practice spread to
those parts of the continental Latin church most influenced by
Celtic missionaries. From the monasteries it spread to the more
earnest secular clergy and laity. As it took its place in proximity to
the surviving remains of the ecclesiastical discipline of public penance, it came often to be substituted for it, with the severity of
the penances imposed by confessors for grave sins reflecting the
standards that had been set in the days of the penitential canons.

In AD 822, when the emperor Louis the Pious undertook a
spectacular public penance, the Schoolmen coined the adage,

'Public penance for public faults, and private penance for private faults'. But this proved to be the death-knell, to all practical purposes, of public penance as a ministry of the Church to penitent and conscience-stricken sinners. Thenceforward the Celtic order of private penance came to be recognized as the universal remedy of the Church for the sins of Christians. At the same time, the clergy were increasingly advocating private penance as a means to personal sanctification. Reforming bishops began to look to it as a sure means to spiritual revival. The movement that aimed at the Christianizing of military force by the creation of orders of chivalry, made auricular confession part of the observances of entry upon knighthood. Thus the ruling classes became familiar with it. Its use is in greatly increased evidence in the twelfth century, when it is the subject of recommendation by a number of local synods. And finally the Fourth Lateran Council of AD 1215 laid obligation on every baptized Christian, when come to years of discretion, to confess once every year.

When the preface to the Commination Service in the Book of Common Prayer declares that the service is to be used 'until the said discipline [of public penance] may be restored again (which is much to be wished)', it may be taken that the eyes of the drafters were upon Calvin's Genevan church order, and not upon the circumstances under which the use of public penance had died out in the medieval Church. Nevertheless, the permanent achievement of the authors of the Commination Service cannot be exaggerated. It should ensure that congregations are kept in mind of the stern face which the Church must ever turn upon the backsliding of Christians. But in effect it was also the covering up of that whole story of the development of private penance that we have been attempting to follow.

To tell the story thus, as if the practice had merely spread, without stimulating fresh thought, and being in turn affected by it, would be but to tell half the truth. For the seventh and eighth centuries, which saw the practice spread over Western Europe, saw also a revival of learning in the Frankish empire in alliance with the papacy, under Charlemagne and his successors. Under Charlemagne's liberal policy, schools were opened in various parts of the empire, where logic and dialectic were taught as concomitants of rhetoric. This gave rise to a revival of reasoned thought, which was accordingly named the Scholastic movement. The intellectual culture to which it gave birth came to be known as Scholasticism.

The logic employed in the schools was the logic of Aristotle, in Latin dress. If the first 'Schoolmen' were accordingly rationalist in method, their aim was anything but destructive. Western Christianity had survived the dark ages largely by dint of conservatism. The Schoolmen therefore started from what was traditional. The Scriptures, the Fathers, and the order established in the Church, formed for them the *datum* of saving knowledge. The aim of their dialectic was to illuminate and extend this knowledge. The *datum* itself was sacrosanct. But in Carolingian times, private penance still lacked the witness of antiquity. The canonists, with the collections of fifth and sixth century penitential canons in their hands, thought it their duty to revive the older discipline. They soon realized the practical impossibility of their task. The Church was no longer concentrated in cities. The continuity of the tradition of public penance had almost everywhere, been broken. The penitential canons, for all their venerable authority, were not fitted to the times. Nevertheless, a synod at Chalons in AD 813 appealed to the emperor to enforce public penance in cases of public scandal. Then, in 822, the dramatic public penance undertaken by the emperor Louis the Pious gave

rise to the adage which ended with these words, 'private penance for private faults', which marks the practical acceptance of
the newer institution. And since the Frankish empire was the chief
power in Western Christendom, Frankish acceptance of the
Celtic practice sealed its acceptance by the whole Western
Church. The reason for much of the hesitation which it encountered was the lack of synodical or other clear authority behind
the books called Penitentials, in use for the guidance of private
penance. What was provided in the Celtic books was a tariff of
penances for sorts of sins, just as much as was the case with the
penitential canons. But the tariffs in the Celtic books were better
fitted to the casuistry of ordinary life in an imperfectly Christian
society. They appealed to the penitent's sense of justice and so
stimulated his penitence. The Penitentials do not aim at being
complete manuals for confessors. It is not made clear how a
private penance was to end. The priest is said to 'heal' the sinner,
who thereupon resumes his Christian life. But no formula of
absolution is given, and it is hard to say when the use of *Absolvo
te* (I absolve thee) began. It is quite possible that it was not until
after the adoption of a General Absolution, answering to a
General Confession at Mass, which first appears about AD 1000,
that absolution in like form, but in the singular, came into use
for the completion of private penance.

At this point we must digress shortly to follow the development of Scholastic thought. The dominance of Augustine in
Western theology ensured that Latin churchmen were familiar
with a Platonic approach to religion. But the teaching of the
liberal arts in the schools now habituated Christian thinkers to
an Aristotelian approach to all questions, not excluding those of
theology. So the ancient tension between Platonic and Aristotelian thought began to be renewed within Scholasticism. But it

was Aristotelianism that was now in the ascendant. First the Spanish successes against their Moorish invaders, and then the contacts of the Crusaders with Greek and Arabic culture, led to a great number of the works of Aristotle, previously unknown to the Latin world, becoming available in Latin translations. The logical rationalism of the early Schoolmen now gave place to an Aristotelian naturalism that gained ground, even in theological discussion, against the supernaturalism of Augustine. Ecclesiastical authority had reason to be uneasy at some developments of Scholasticism. But the main body of Christian thinkers remained loyal to Church tradition, while striving to render that tradition more intelligible with the aid of their new means and incentives to study. The outcome of these later developments can be studied, as regards the doctrine of the forgiveness of sins, in the *Sentences* of Peter Lombard, Archbishop of Paris a generation before the Lateran Council of 1215. The *Sentences* (*Sententiae*, opinions) form an ordered collection of the judgments of approved Fathers of the Church upon every main subject of Christian belief. Peter treats all these opinions as authoritative, and labours to harmonize them when they appear to be in conflict. But this necessity arises, not so much from real contradictions in the citations, but rather from the tendency of the age to take sides, as between naturalism and supernaturalism. So it appears that Peter is not simply recording, but rather is interpreting the Fathers to the men of his own generation. Thus, when he has recorded the patristic teaching that Second Repentance is unrepeatable, he comments that Second Repentance is for *crimina*, but for other sins repentance is essentially repeatable. So he cites Ambrose *On Repentance* to the effect[1] that 'Penitence may be defined as mourning evil deeds that are past beyond un-

[1] Bk IV, Dist. 14–17 (Ambrose, Nicene and Post-Nicene Fathers X, 1894).

doing, and committing the like no more'. Peter points out that only the present passing moment lies within the power of the human will. It is therefore unthinkable that pardon should be witheld until the penitent shall have proved sinless to the last. Present pardon must crown present resolve. What is requisite for absolution is that, at the moment when it is to be pronounced, the sinner should be in the mind never, in will or deed, to repeat his sin. The aim of penance is to cut at the root of the sin. Its moral effectiveness is more important than its severity.

Peter goes on to say that if absolution is followed by a repetition of the same sin, it does not prove that the penitence was vain. It brought hallowing for a time, which, though lost, is ready to revive at a subsequent conversion. And even if, at the time of being absolved, the penitent's intention was defective, that very defect can be made the subject of later repentance. Peter's mind is evidently no longer upon the extinct discipline of public penance, to which his patristic citations had reference, but upon the private penance in use in the twelfth century and assumed to be generally repeatable. In the older discipline, something incidental in the sphere of nature drew with it something of eternal validity in the sphere of grace. It appears to Peter that this is equally true of private penance. It has its parts in nature: as regards the penitent, in secret confession to a priest, made with true penitence and with willing acceptance of the penance assigned; on the side of the priest, in assessing the penance and in pronouncing absolution. Its supernatural part is the restoration of the sinner to perfect innocence. Therefore Peter names such penance a sacrament and makes it one of seven such operations in the Church.

Peter next asks if contrition wins forgiveness without use of the sacrament of penance. He musters patristic opinions in favour of an affirmative answer. But he then appeals to the Aristotelian principle of correspondence between the outward and the inward. Unless, he says, something in nature opposes an obstacle, contrition ought to direct a man to the use of the sacrament of penance. The former answer, therefore, serves only to reassure those who, through no fault of their own, cannot have the sacramental ministry of penance. All should seek the sacrament of penance when it can be had, because the very fact of seeking it annuls that element of deliberation and contumacy which is the worst part of the sin. And when the sin is deadly (a *crimen*), then the fact of seeking penance at once reduces it to the status of a venial or involuntary sin. Therefore, Peter concludes, negligence with regard to going to confession is neglect of one's soul, even though the sins upon one's conscience are all venial. Thus he labours to accumulate incentives to use what he has thus set forth as a sacrament, without surrendering the principle that the essence of penitence is to be an interior motion. He does not (as Augustine did) reject fear as an incentive to seek penance. Under the circumstances of the twelfth century, very unformed Christians, if driven by fear to the priest in confession, might well be taught and converted on their way to absolution. In this case, though fear had been the incentive at first, it would not be so throughout.

This vigorous commendation of private penance by the Lombard was made at a time when society looked up to the Church as never before or since. And under those circumstances, private penance appeared as a great and effective means in the hands of the clergy for converting and hallowing their people, and the step taken by the Lateran Council in 1215 is understandable.

During the thirteenth century, Aristotle's *Metaphysics*, now known in the West for the first time, fired Scholastic theologians to apply syllogistic reasoning to the whole range of the Christian revelation. This movement found its crowning achievement in the *Summa Theologica*[1] of Thomas Aquinas, whose activities extended from 1251 to 1274. In this immense work of ingenuity and learning, the author examines opinions that have been held with regard to every subdivision of every article of the Christian faith. Over ten thousand opinions investigated in the *Summa* are rejected, in the course of arriving at those oracular statements, beginning *Respondeo dicendum quod*, which give the Thomist conclusion on each several point. Unfortunately the forgiveness of sins was one of the last subjects to be broached, and Aquinas died before he had finished his treatment of it. But, as he opens the subject, he brings us face to face with the characteristic weakness of Scholastic theology. This is that it witholds rational criticism from anything that has enjoyed immemorial acceptance in the Church. In Jerome's Latin rendering of Matt. 4.17, the words used to translate 'repent' are *poenitentiam agite* (do penance). Whatever the reason he had had for this rendering, by the thirteenth century it was sacrosanct. Therefore 'Do penance', taken as a dominical command, was the starting point, with Aquinas, for the Christian doctrine of the forgiveness of sins. With such a start, Aquinas went on to interpret Luke 24.47, where the apostles are commanded by Christ to preach repentance in all the world, as the dominical institution of the sacrament of penance, as that had been set forth by Peter Lombard. Thus forgiveness of sins is now taken, in the *Summa*, to have no practical existence apart from the sacrament of penance. Aquinas disposes of the opinion that divine pardon can be had apart from the sacrament of penance, by saying that a man in sin cannot obtain for himself charity, faith and repentance. Therefore even if the

[1] Literally translated by Fathers of the English Dominican Province, 22 vols., 2nd and revised ed., 1923. See note p. 106 below.

opinion can be justified in theory, it cannot be in practice. Aquinas fits penance into his scheme of sacraments by calling what the penitent does 'the matter', and the priestly absolution 'the form', of the sacrament. Plainly, sin cannot be the 'matter' of a sacrament. But there cannot be penance without sin. So Aquinas defines sin as 'the matter of the matter'. But if this is a difficulty, the priestly pronouncing of the now established formula *Absolvo te* fits without difficulty into the idea of a sacrament. It is an act in space and time which at once signifies and effects the eternal reality of divine pardon.

Aquinas disposes of the rigorist opinion that some penance is unrepeatable by branding it heresy. He interprets Heb. 10.26 as meaning that baptism is unrepeatable, with the implication that penance is not. But deplorable as much of the discussion is, down to this point, Aquinas has valuable things to say when he comes to analyse penitence. He finds first a revulsion of shame, just as if the sin had been committed at that moment. This emotion achieves the otherwise impossible result of bringing the sin back, out of the past, into the present. And in the second place he finds a dispassionate condemnation of the sin in the mind of the penitent, as he contemplates it, as it were, from a distance. Aquinas observes that in Purgatory we shall be capable only of this detached condemnation of our sins. But while we live in the flesh, with its capacity for shame, our burning condemnation of what we have done may turn into a rational hunger and thirst after righteousness, by which we shall be taken beyond the resolve not to sin again, and moved to offer works of obedience in reparation to the offended holiness of God. Aquinas says that the natural man when he recoils from his sin, cannot get beyond servile fear. Only when the Church aids his impotence can he be recovered to a state of grace, and make effective repentance. But it is for the devout Christian also, to seek the aid of the Church, out of pure piety and devotion to God's righteousness, in repenting for those venial sins which are unavoidable and involve no turning away from God. However, in his last days, Aquinas seems to have been less content to make so clear a distinction between classes of sinners. Considering that penitence is always the beginning of righteousness and that it is the nature of any good action that it should not stop until it has reached completion, Aquinas came to hold that, whatever the sin, repentance must go forward by the same succession of stages, defined by Chrysostom: contrition in the heart, confession in the mouth, and a final making of full amends. This was to make the forgiveness of sins still less than before separable from the sacrament of penance, to which Aquinas supposed I John 5.16 to refer, excluding from its operation only the sin against the Holy Ghost.

Thus the triumphant progress of the Celtic institution of private penance had ended in its complete domination of the Latin half of the Church. By the thirteenth century, it was of immemorial antiquity. Its origins had been long out of mind. The dialectic of the Schoolmen had established, to their satisfaction, that private penance is a sacrament ordained by Christ. It must therefore be construed as part of the revelation of God made in Christ, and so must be taken to express and effect all that we can know of God's will to grant men the forgiveness of their sins.

Note: Penance is treated in the third Part of the *Summa*, headed *De Sacramentis*, Quaestiones 84–90. Aquinas had planned three more Quaestiones.

CHAPTER NINE

Salvation by Faith

MARTIN LUTHER, although he lived two and a half centuries after Aquinas, was not acquainted with his *Summa Theologica*. He was brought up on the much more recent *Commentary on the Sentences*, by Gabriel Biel, co-founder of the University of Tübingen. The universal acceptance of Aquinas was only to come later, after Pius V had declared him a 'Doctor of the Church' in 1567. The important thing, for our purpose, about Biel, is that he was a Nominalist. The inevitable clash of Aristotelian and Platonic principles, in Scholasticism, produced a series of radical Aristotelians who denied to universals any reality outside the human imagination. As, therefore, declaring universals to be mere names and not existent things, these thinkers were called Nominalists. But as theologians they were confronted with a difficulty. A doctrine such as that of the Incarnation cannot be stated without implying the real existence of universals. That doctrine, for example, requires that not only do individual men exist, but that, in the mind of God, they form mankind, so that mankind is no mere child of the human imagination, but, as thought by God, is as real an entity as each and every individual that goes to compose it. The existence of this entity of universal character, Nominalist theologians would say, was not to be known by nature, but is, through the Incarnation, revealed to faith. Thus Nominalism, as it advanced, made an ever sharper division between natural knowledge received by reason, and revelation received by faith. An orthodox Nominalist like Biel believed that natural knowledge and revelation, though unconfused, fit together without conflict. In practice there were, in Biel's presentation of Christian doctrine, gaping seams between the natural and revealed. But these logical incoherences in Biel would probably never have arrested Luther's attention, apart from the spiritual crisis that came to him. It was Scholasticism, however, as represented to Luther by Biel, that was responsible for the crisis in Luther's life.

Luther had joined the Augustinian Friars in 1505, and soon after was sent to the house of the Order connected with the newly founded University of Wittenberg. Here he reached the grade of Doctor in 1511. At this time he had conceived no quarrel with Scholasticism. But it was typical of the confidence in its own powers which Scholasticism had developed that it was not content to say what must be thought. It was ready to prophesy what, in the spiritual life, must happen. In particular, Scholastic theologians declared that any contrite sinner who had recourse to the sacrament of penance, would receive grace; by which they meant that some supernatural gift would come to him, whereby he would be able to do good works, and make progress in sanctification. Luther took this assurance most seriously, frequented the confessional and received repeatedly counsel, penance and absolution. But the progressive elimination of concupiscence, for which he longed and had been led to hope, did not follow. A long time passed, in which self-disgust and superstitious fear drove him deeper and deeper into despair. Meanwhile his director continued to preach to him the quest of virtue. His own feelings taught him to dread the holiness of God. He heard no word preached that encouraged him to trust in God's will to forgive and save. The optimism of Biel, who taught that free will and reason were but little impaired through the Fall, and that therefore a Catholic, with the help of the sacraments, ought to be able to overcome the disorder in the lower faculties of the soul, seemed to Luther to mock his impotence. It appeared to him that, all unchecked by his recourse to penance, an infernal force of evil in himself was separating him from his Creator, and even driving him to hate where he was commanded to love.

From this desperate condition, Luther was delivered, as by a flash of light, by Rom. 1.17, where he read that there was revealed in the Gospel 'a righteousness of God by faith (that is, the faith of Jesus in his Father) unto faith' (that is, leading to faith in the believer); 'as it is written, But the righteous shall live by faith'. With this he joined John 1.16, 'Of his fulness we all received, and grace (that is, God's favour falls on us) for grace' (that is, on account of the favour that God has towards his Son). So it burst upon Luther that what God was demanding of him was not virtue (which he despaired of attaining), but faith. God does not look for intrinsic righteousness in man. He has found the sole human intrinsic righteousness in Christ, perfected in his sacrifice upon the cross. But to these who throw themselves by faith upon that righteousness, extrinsic in relation to themselves, God imputes it as if it were in them. This then, is forgiveness of sins: that God imputes to us, when we believe and, so believing, truly repent, Christ's righteousness, instead of our intrinsic sins. Where God imputes righteousness, the Holy Spirit returns, though formerly driven forth by sin. So the fruits of the Spirit produce themselves in the life of a believer. These fruits are, in fact, virtues. But they do not make the believer virtuous, because they flow from his Redeemer, living in a hidden manner within him. If men judge the believer to have become holy and righteous, what they behold is altogether God's doing. And if anyone could be holy and righteous in any other way, it would be neither holiness nor righteousness, but sin. Luther's new realization of the Gospel began to be made public when, as Friar Doctor, he gave, in 1515, a course of lectures in the University on the Epistle to the Romans. In his *Scholion* on the citation of Ps. 32,vv. 1 and 2, in Rom. 4.7f, Luther asks 'Who are these blessed to whom the Lord imputes no sin?' He answers, out of the closing verse of Ps. 68. The sense of the Hebrew is, 'O God, thou art terrible out of thy holy places'. But the Latin Vulgate rendered it, 'God is wonderful in his saints'. The wonder, Luther explains, is that these saints are intrinsically sinners and will be such until the end. But they are the blessed to whom God remits their iniquities and covers their sins. The Vulgate mistranslation is immaterial. It merely opened the way for Luther to express his new recognition that a Christian is a saint and a sinner at one and the same time.

Luther had learned from Biel the antithesis of faith and reason, of revelation and natural knowledge. But he now perceived that, in place of the Christian Gospel, the Schoolmen were teaching the pagan aretology of Aristotle, with no more veneer of Christianity than could be imparted with the words, 'With the help of the sacraments of the Church'. It was of course penance, particularly, that was regarded, in the ecclesiastical world, as Christianizing the quest of personal virtue and holiness. This was the teaching that Luther had striven so hard to follow. And now he found it to be false and unchristian. He who believes the Gospel, Luther said, must renounce the hope and desire for intrinsic righteousness. So he waxed in bitterness towards the doctrine of the Schoolmen, seeing that the more successfully anyone were to follow it, the more he and others would be duped into accepting as righteousness that which God knew for none of his. They were thus leading men back to the abrogated law, and again making men proud of good works. But under this specious righteousness, concupiscence flourishes and bears fruit ceaselessly in actual, even if secret, sinning. The worst invention of the Schoolmen, in Luther's eyes, was the doctrine that good works, as measured by the law, draw down infallibly, to aid their doer, a *gratia de congruo* (goodness given in answer to goodness), as though natural goodness was akin to the righteousness of God. Here Luther laid his finger upon the tendency of the Schoolmen to think of grace as a gift, a creature-power separable in thought from the Giver, and appropriable by the human individual privileged to receive it, together with its fruits. These things, Luther says, should never have been taught. God indeed gives good gifts to men, but if we put our trust in them, they cease to be blessings and become snares. Indeed, *aversio a Deo per conversionem ad creaturas* was the Scholastic definition of mortal sin! On the other hand, there are things they should have taught, which they had buried under silence. We are full of concupiscence. The law of God says, Thou shalt not lust! (Rom. 7.7): concupiscence is therefore sinful. Manifestly it is the kindling for actual sins. Concupiscence is part of our fallen nature. God does not quench it in his saints lest they, like the Schoolmen, who fancied it all but quenched, should delude themselves into taking a spurious self-righteousness for the object of God's favour. God therefore leaves concupiscence rooted in us, so that we may never be blinded to the fact that our salvation remains wholly his free gift. When we embrace forgiveness on this understanding, we begin to seek what is good, for God's glory and not our own; and not as though we had power to attain it, but only faith to receive it. Therefore, said Luther, confessors ought to expend all their counsel on moving penitents to faith, while preachers, instead of holding up for imitation the achievements of saints, and magnifying in us the wretched remnants of reason and free-will, ought to be moving men to put their whole trust in God's free gift of righteousness, by imputation now, and by fruition hereafter.

It is evident that, in Luther's teaching on the forgiveness of sins, the emphasis is on faith. There is, however, a place for repentance, though by no means so spectacular. Luther did not account as Christian penitence the torments of servile fear through which he had passed before he received his apprehension of the Gospel. That was fear such as the natural man entertains, when his mind is enough enlightened for him to conceive the wrath of God merited by his sins. It is an emotion devoid of charity and is to be accounted sin, rather than a motion towards escape from sin. But when faith is born, the believer sees his sins with a sorrow devoid of fear, which is a fruit of the Spirit, a sorrow in which the sinner's passing of judgment on his sins redounds to the glory of God. Such a sorrow may well move a Christian to make confession to a minister of the Gospel. But this confessor, Luther says, must not sit as judge of the satisfaction due, lest he usurp the place of the Holy Spirit. The true work of the minister in the confessional, according to Luther, is to evoke and strengthen faith. The evoking of penitence will follow naturally, as the believer, enlightened by the Holy Spirit, contemplates himself as sinner.

The opposite of faith, in Luther's experience, consists in the torturing doubts and scruples that he had himself known so well. Therefore he advised penitents to avoid solitude and to abstain from self-punishing austerities, but instead to throw their reliance upon the fact of their having been absolved, and to seek Christian

companionship. 'We preachers absolve', Luther said, and told a
penitent to say, when assailed by doubts, 'Begone, devil, for I am
absolved.' Such is Luther's teaching on confession. But the confessional has not, in fact, kept its place in Lutheran practice.

What we most miss in the Lutheran treatment of repentance is
any reference to a resolve, on the part of the penitent, to sin no
more. The reason is that Luther had an almost morbid fear of
human presumption in quest of virtue. We might say that
Luther's faith did good works before it thought of them, since he
feared that to think of them would at once vitiate them as fruits
of faith. This fear was not rational. There is no reason why the
planning of future good works should not be, and be welcomed
as, inspired by the Holy Spirit, or that the works so planned
should not be a pure offering to the glory of God. Luther's
avoidance of the subject of good resolutions, with its counter-
part in a furious negation of all human dignity, worth and great-
ness, is an exaggeration of ideas that are truly Augustinian; an
exaggeration into which Christendom has almost unanimously
refused to be led.

On the other hand, Luther was Augustinian in his concept of
the two dominical sacraments as predestined instruments of divine
action in and through the Church on earth. It was a principle,
with Luther, that God does nothing by halves. Therefore, in
baptism, he gives total remission of original sin and all committed
actual sins; and this in spite of the fact that concupiscence remains, though with the baptismal gift of the Spirit to work
against it. Thus in baptism a child of wrath becomes, in God's
sight, an immaculate child of grace, and the sins which in fact
continue to flow from his vitiated nature are all venial. Luther
made no difference in the application of these principles to infant
baptism, of which he upheld the use.

H

Luther was driven by the needs of an anti-papal polemic to emphasize the liberty of the Christian man against the claims of hierarchical government and ecclesiastical institutions. Thus he failed to exhibit the Church alongside Scripture and the two sacraments, as an instrument of God's action on earth. But the movement of liberation from ecclesiastical authority which he had started was not to reach a standstill. Zwingli and the Anabaptists between them discarded the view of the sacraments as predestined means of divine action in the Church on earth, and reduced them to the status of scriptural tokens of human faith. Protestant radicalism thus forced Luther to discover how much, after all, he remained an ecclesiastical man. He still believed the Church to be God's instrument for the communication of his spiritual gifts to believing people, primarily by the living Word preached by a legitimate ministry, but also by the sacraments, as infusing a leaven of godliness to counteract the corruption which persists in those who, by faith, have become saints. At the time when Luther thus began to recover his Augustinian doctrine of the Church, he was already both excommunicate from Rome and a proscribed person by decree of the emperor Charles V. On the other hand, he and his cause were under the protection of Protestant princes. When, therefore, in 1526, the Turkish victory at Mohacs laid Hungary open to their invasion, and the military unity of the empire became of vital importance, Charles called the Protestant princes to Augsburg in an attempt to reach some religious understanding. Here, in 1530, Lutheran theologians, led by Philip Melancthon, presented a statement of Protestant doctrine which has come to be known as the Augsburg Confession,[1] and to be regarded as the fundamental formulation

[1] In B. J. Kidd, *Documents illustrative of the Continental Reformation*, 1911, No. 116.

of Lutheranism. In this Confession, Articles III, IV and XII are
concerned specifically with the forgiveness of sins. In Article III,
the typical Lutheran expression, that 'we are reconciled to the
Father' by Christ, is replaced by the more traditional teaching
that the Father is reconciled to us. Luther had pictured the sinless Christ as tempted by the devil to despair of us and to disidentify himself from us. This he steadfastly refused to do, and
suffered to the utmost without hating either God or men. Faith,
Luther concluded, enables us to identify ourselves with him, so
as to be no longer estranged from God. Luther, in short, looked
at the question from the side of man the estranged. At Augsburg,
the other side of the relationship was put first. The Lutheran
theologians there said that, through the atonement made by
Christ, the Father can identify us with his Son and disidentify us
from our sins. The Father's non-imputation to us of our sins, to
use Luther's phrase, would be a fiction, were it not for the reality
of the work of Christ. The Confession got rid of the awkward
term 'non-imputation', by employing instead the positive and
scriptural phrase, 'imputing of righteousness', and showed it to
be the real and logical consequence of Christ's death, whereby,
in the traditional phrase, he reconciled the Father to us. The
Article also made prudent retreat from Luther's confusion of
concupiscence, which dies with the body, and original sin, which
does not. It made a further escape from the subjectivity of Luther's
expressions by seeing the fruits of atonement actualized in the
Church, as in the gift of the ascended Lord to men, whereby the
members of that Church, severally, receive the indwelling of the
Holy Spirit. In this way, the Article achieved a much less vulner-
able formulation of the Lutheran faith than might be gathered
out of Luther's writings.

Article IV claims for Christ's death a monopoly in the making of *satisfactio* for sins. Medieval theologians had given the word *satisfactio* a legalistic sense, as meaning payment of the price due, of which they considered a part to consist of the pains suffered by sinners in penance. The Lutherans at Augsburg took *satisfactio* in the medieval sense, but repudiated any ability on the part of sinners to contribute to it. Without sufficient reason, they included in what they thus repudiated the asceticism, including the vows of poverty, chastity and obedience, that formed the foundation of the life of the religious Orders. A consequence was that this Article, in which the Lutherans made their nearest approach to a Scholastic outlook, did most to establish the impossibility of reconciliation between the two sides of the Augsburg Diet. The rift was completed by Article XX, which asserts that assurance of forgiveness follows whenever faith in the Gospel enables a frightened conscience to realize that God is placated towards it (on the basis of Rom. 5.1). Thus the absolution which, according to Article XII, upon the sinner's repentance, the Church gives instantly and as often as need be, is nothing else than a preaching-with-assurance of the Gospel. Thus, against such an ecclesiastical transaction as the so-called Sacrament of Penance, the Augsburg Confession made canonical the Lutheran 'evangelical experience' ('We know ourselves forgiven when we believe ourselves the objects of the divine favour in Christ') and so asserted something that was in danger of becoming subjective, unless all weight were thrown upon the abiding word of Scripture. On the other hand, there can be little doubt that the Lutherans suspected anyone who did not profess to have shared the 'evangelical experience' of being pagan at heart.

From the close of the Diet of Augsburg, Lutheranism became a great religious cause, furnished with a coherent body of doctrine, confronting the continued existence of Roman Catholicism,

As a consequence, Christendom stood more profoundly divided than ever before. And the question from which the division most resulted was that of the means of assurance of the forgiveness of sins.

CHAPTER TEN

Trent and after

TEN years after Augsburg, the Company of Jesus, conceived and brought into being by Ignatius Loyola, received papal sanction as a new religious Order. It typified a revival of personal piety, within the Roman obedience, that had been stirring from early in the century. It now gathered force, within that obedience, in answer to the challenge of Lutheranism. The whole movement has come to be known by the title of the Counter-reformation. With the renewal of prestige which the papal cause drew from its Counter-reformation, the frontiers between the two religious confessions began to be stabilized, with Roman Catholicism in possession of Southern Europe, and the Protestant bodies equally established over Northern Europe, including the British Isles. But the loosening effects of Lutheran teaching were being felt within the Roman Catholic Church. At the same time, the cohesion of the Protestant cause constituted a challenge only to be met by an impressive statement and justification of Roman Catholic doctrine. The General Council of Constance in the early fifteenth century, held in an attempt to reform and unite the Church, had left in circulation two distinct ideas concerning General Councils. One was that a General Council called by the Pope is the appropriate means for bringing to expression the mind of the Catholic Church. The other was that agreement reached by such a Council would bind the Pope. It was the second of these ideas that explains the appeal of Luther, as early as 1518, for the submission of his cause to a General Council. As a result of this, the Protestant princes of Germany continued to press the emperor for the calling of such a Council. It was, of course, in their minds that Protestant theologians should be heard in their own defence by a General Council of the Church. The emperor was eager to content the Lutheran states, and in 1545 Pope Paul III agreed to call a General Council, with its venue at Trent, in the Tyrol. This was on the Southern side of the confessional frontier. Moreover the Pope summoned only appropriate persons acknowledging his jurisdiction, leaving the representatives of Protestantism to make their appearance, as defendants, under imperial safe-conduct. When the Council assembled, in 1545, it inspired the Protestants with so little confidence that no representatives of their cause were sent to it. Accordingly the Council, in sessions extending from 1545 to 1547, so far judged the defendants in their absence as to formulate Roman Catholic doctrine in answer to the teaching of Luther and other Protestants. New pressure for the fulfilment of the desire of the Protestant states led to the appearance at Trent of theological representatives of the Protestant princes, when the Council sat again in 1551–2. These representatives claimed that the whole work of the earlier sessions constituted a prejudgment of their cause, and demanded retrial *ab initio*. This was refused, and equally, in a renewed sitting of the Council, 1562–3, there was no attempt at conciliation. In short, the whole work of the Council was directed to the doctrinal consolidation of the Roman Catholic cause, in opposition to the doctrines and Church orders that had established themselves under the Protestant Reformation.

An early part of the work of the Council was to define Roman

Catholic teaching on the forgiveness of sins, in such wise as to brand as heretical the Lutheran doctrine of the imputation of righteousness to sinners, and of sanctification through faith without regard to works. The Council did not succeed in disengaging itself from Lutheran ground in this matter, asserting, in reply, the principle of 'double righteousness', against the ultra-Augustinianism of Luther. The principle of 'double righteousness' requires belief that the forgiven receive not only the imputation to them of the righteousness of Christ but also a gift of spiritual power enabling them to attain actual righteousness. To say this was to cleave to the Scholastic notion of grace as a gift separable in thought from the Person of the Holy Spirit himself, and constituting a possession of the Christian as an individual.

Next the Council had to refute Luther's doctrine that the concupiscence which baptism does not efface is sin. After admitting that this concupiscence owes its origin to Adam's sin, and itself leads to sin, the Council asserted that when St Paul calls it sin, he uses the word loosely. This concupiscence is so far from actually being sin that its persistence in the elect provides the very arena whereon they gain their victory. The Council asserted the Nominalist doctrine that human free will was only maimed, and not destroyed, by the Fall, and declared the Virgin Mary exempt from even that disability. It stated that free-will, even in its maimed state, is roused by the call of God to ally itself with those good impulses which he sends us, and that such co-operation of our free will, especially by prayer, is indispensable to the working out of our salvation; which salvation we thereafter owe wholly to God. The Council admitted that sanctity is insecure in every elect person so long as he lives in the flesh, but proclaimed the sufficiency of the sacrament of penance to recover the fallen, so that the attainment of actual sanctity never becomes impossible.

Because of his human insecurity, however, neglect to use penance is a courting of damnation.

The leader in this moderate Augustinian formulation was the Superior of the Augustinian Friars, Jerome Seripando, destined to die during the close of the Council, in 1563, while presiding as Papal Legate and Cardinal. But from the time that the Council reassembled in 1551, the new Jesuit Order was represented there by Father Laynez. In his person the temper of the Counter-reformation made itself felt, in a rising confidence in the power of the Church, as the instrument of God for the forwarding of our salvation. This is testified by the fruits of actual righteousness in the faithful. Laynez disparaged the doctrine of 'double righteousness', set forth by Seripando, as Semi-Lutheran. He appealed to a saying of Augustine, that when God crowns our merits, he crowns what was of his own giving. This, Laynez said, implied that God wills to provide us with a righteousness that shall be ours. In this way, Laynez revealed the tendency of his Order, as compared with other Roman Catholic theologians, to move still further from pure Augustinianism.

It had been a fundamental conviction of the founder of the Order that heroic virtue is a goal which God has put within the reach of man, even in this present life, and that he calls us to seek it by all the means with which he has endowed his Church. Accordingly the Jesuits took a view of human endeavour which may (though not without qualifications) be called Semi-Pelagian. Other Roman Catholic theologians of the time almost equalled the Reformers by their Augustinianism. Consequently, at this stage, the 'Semi-Pelagianism' that characterized the Jesuits tended to become a party badge betokening the stoutest anti-Protestant orthodoxy.

After the Council was over, this tendency was to find

further expression in a development of teaching upon the sacrament of penance. At the Council, the part of the penitent, in this sacrament, was defined as being contrition, so that a duty lies upon the priest to satisfy himself, before giving absolution, that the penitent is contrite for his sins. It would have given rise to a grave division in the Council if this statement had there been challenged. Nevertheless, there were many who desired to see it modified, so as to exalt the power of the Church to give aid to all but impenitent sinners, through the sacrament of penance. The idea was not new. Scholastic discussion of the part of the penitent in the sacrament of penance had concerned itself, as early as the twelfth century, to determine what was the least degree of penitence that might justify the granting of absolution. When the question was posed in this form, it was seen that it was rather the quality than the quantity of feeling that made penitence Christian. Fear can produce a seeming penitence without there being any appreciable concern, on the sinner's part, for the glory of God, as the end of repentance. In other words, such seeming penitence might proceed from self-interest unmixed with charity. The word contrition, which pictures the heart of the sinner as broken, and literally 'reduced to powder', was clearly meant to be a strong word, implying that the contrite penitent was moved by a lively and loving sorrow for having offended against the holiness of God. Confessors knew, however, that many who sought absolution did so because the Church had taught them to fear the consequences of dying unabsolved, but had not succeeded in teaching them to care for the glory of God in any personal way.

Accordingly the word attrition, implying only that the hard heart of the sinner has been made so far to feel his sin as to be no longer impenitent, was coined, and is first found in this connection in the writings of Alain of Lille (1128–1203). The Nominalist school, with its emphasis upon the partial survival of free-will, held that attrition, even when the traces of the love of God were almost imperceptible, began to separate the sinner from his sin. That being so, the completion of the sacrament of penance must ensure a movement of the will of the penitent towards the love of God. Therefore the priest should urge an attrite sinner towards contrition by every means in his power, but should not, by refusing absolution, throw him backwards. He must consider that the attrite sinner does not yet realize the insufficiency of his penitence, but that he is likely to do so, under kind handling.

Since it was in the Nominalist tradition that Luther grew up, it seemed to him, after his conversion, that such a promise of future righteousness to a man who feared God only as the devils fear him, was blasphemous. And it was, in fact, in answer to Luther's outright expression of this sentiment in his *Sermon on Penance* that the Council of Trent replied, word for word, insisting on the utility, without asserting the sufficiency, of the revulsion of fear and shame on the part of a sinner for his sins.

It was, of course, clear that all the powers of the Church could not reconcile the blankly impenitent. But after the Council a quest began for the right expression to distinguish, from a merely self-interested grief, an attrition in which there was some element of charity. Cardinal Cajetan said that if the penitent preferred the glory of God before the desire of repeating his sin, attrition had opened the way towards contrition. The *Catechism of Trent*, 1566, invested with something of official status, found repentance to be true if there were unselfish regret arising upon the remembrance of God. But, equally with the formularies of the Council, the *Catechism* avoided actual use of the word attrition. In 1567, however, an ultra-Augustinian theologian who took part in the Council, Michael Baius of Louvain, suffered the condemnation of some of his theses. This prepared the way for Suarez, and other theologians of the University of Salamanca, to move in the Semi-Pelagian direction. They sustained the opinion that the more probable interpretation of the rulings of Trent would be expressed in the words, *satis est attritio agnita* (meaning that a confessor can absolve when he recognizes the presence of attrition). This started an attack, by the attritionists, upon those who still demanded contrition in penance. The contritionists replied. The dispute went on until, in 1667, Pope Alexander VII forbade either side to attack the other.

Meanwhile the tendency has been to assume, in Roman Catholic discussion of the sufficiency of attrition, that whatever motives of self-interest there may be involved, no one comes to penance without some element of regard for God. This act of piety, small as it is, would, theoretically, call forth a *gratia de congruo*, even apart from the sacrament of penance. *A fortiori*, a confession made with attrition will lead to contrition, whereupon absolution can rightly be given, and righteousness will be restored. What underlies the *a fortiori* is the conception of penance as a sacrament, *ex opere operato* enacting what it expresses. In a sacrament, as long as the appropriate form and matter are present, the might of God is pledged to the attainment of the end to which the sacrament was ordained. In penance, only impenitence can defeat the attainment of divine pardon.

This fine-spun Scholastic reasoning was, as we have seen, begun long before the Reformation. But in the Tridentine and Post-tridentine emphasis upon the sacramental character of penance, and its consequences, the influence of reaction from Lutheran teaching is predominant. And in the doctrinal movement that has been described we see the interest, characteristic of the Counter-reformation, in magnifying the supernatural powers of the Church entrusted to the priesthood. From the point of view of theological reasoning, the whole movement remains within the tradition of medieval Scholasticism, in that it carries on trains of deductive reasoning which are left unrelated to the developing world of fact. Not that the Post-tridentine Church of Rome was out of touch with its actual world, which had become one that required the priesthood, if it were to keep its hold upon the people of the Roman Catholic countries, often to woo where it had formerly commanded. Thus, if folk of tepid piety were treated too drastically, as, for example, by being refused absolution for reasons that offended them, they might pass out of control. This made it expedient, when such folk submit themselves voluntarily to the discipline of the Church, to be able to meet their expectations.

This is what the maxim *satis est attritio agnita* ensures. Priests warn the people that if they die in mortal sin, they will go to hell, and that the longer they put off coming to penance, when they are aware of mortal sin, the greater is the danger. They must come to confession before Easter, so as to be admitted to their Easter communion. And the consequence of such a combination of warnings is that that part of the flock that most needs converting comes to the confessional at a season when penitents are waiting in queues to be heard. So the attrite make their confession, it may be to a priest to whom they are not intimately known, under conditions which make impracticable any use of the confessional for evangelism. As he listens, it must become clear to the priest that the so-called penitent is not contrite. All that he can then do, in the time at his disposal, is to try and make sure that the sorrow manifested in the confession is not the sorrow of the impenitent; that is to say, that the thing that has brought the person to the confessional is something more Christian than annoyance and shame that his way of life is not held in esteem in the Church. But, if the so-called penitent is in fact impenitent; if he is merely answering to social pressures, and not to any genuinely religious impulse; he will produce every obstacle to the unmasking of his hypocrisy. The priest must be very acute if he is not to be driven to giving him the benefit of the doubt, so as to assume his state to be one of attrition, and proceed to absolution. Then, should the sinner have been hiding impenitence (and in this case he is likely to have deceived himself before he deceives the confessor), the sacrament of penance fails through absence of the necessary matter, namely the repentance of the sinner. As often as this happens, there is an appearance of sin having been forgiven, but the actuality is a condoning of sin, combining with the commission of a further grievous sin. This is obviously a great evil. But it may be argued that, with a vigilant clergy, the number of such cases will be small, while the policy that keeps the confessional well in use, by every class of sinner, ensures that the number of sinners who are, by faith and penitence, reconciled to God, is very great.

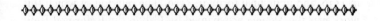

CHAPTER ELEVEN

Reassessments

WHILE the Roman Catholics were making their reassessment of their heritage from the Schoolmen, on the other side of the confessional frontier, a reassessment of Luther's teaching was going on. The Lutheran cause, in spite of sharp persecution from the government of Francis I, was infiltrating into France. It drew in a young Frenchman, originally destined for the priesthood, but starting a career in law, Jean Calvin. In 1529 he underwent a 'spiritual conversion'. Unlike Luther, Calvin did not record the form of his experience. He had already accepted the doctrine that faith is the only door to salvation. The tenor of his after-life would suggest that he came to believe that he had a special mission from God to reform the Church according to primitive purity. But in Calvin we do not at all see a man leaning upon an experience in the past, nor upon something in which he feels himself singular. If he came, at a certain point, to believe himself elect to salvation, he believed that the continuing token of election, for others as for himself, is the indwelling of the Holy Spirit. A signal proof of this is that heart and mind kindle to the meaning of Scripture, seeing that the Holy Spirit is the Author of that meaning. The restoration of the Church to primitive purity, agreed by all to be necessary, Calvin conceived to lie in bringing all Christian life to the measure of Scripture. Calvin set himself to supply a *Summa* of Christian doctrine and Church order on these lines, and achieved this task in his *Institutes of the Christian Religion*,[1] first appearing in 1536, and in its final form, in 1559. The religion of which this work was the *Summa* was named by Calvin the Reformed Religion, and all bodies that have embraced the Calvinist system call themselves Reformed churches. Apart from Scripture, Calvin was well read in Augustine, from whom he took with avidity just that which Augustine reached most reluctantly, that the human race is damned, except for some whom an inexplicable election predestines to salvation. Calvin so underlined original sin that it became, in his teaching, total depravity. That is to say that, since the Fall, man's free-will is powerless, except to make for himself an existence alienated from God. But, Calvin continued, the mercy and loving-kindness of God come to expression in his will to redeem some from suffering that eternal punishment which is due in satisfaction to his holiness. We cannot know why this or that person is redeemed from the eternity of hell and elect to eternal life. It is true that the elect all believe the Gospel. But they are not elect because they believe. Rather, they cannot help believing, because they are elect. The elect are sinners, like all other men, and by nature unforgivable. But God gives the gift of faith, by which they are moved to repentance, and so, becoming forgivable, are forgiven. Thus, said Calvin, to whom God forgives anything, he forgives everything. Forgiveness does not put an end to penitence, but, on the contrary, one continuing sign of election is that a Christian should be as continually repenting his sins. What enables him to repent is faith in the Gospel, and it is likewise the Gospel that gives assurance of forgiveness, in that the believer recognizes by faith that Christ died for his sins.

Repentance does not earn forgiveness, but it is the appointed

[1] Translated by H. Beveridge, 1845, 3 vols; to be published shortly in Library of Christian Classics (XX, XXI). Forgiveness is treated in Bk III c. 4.

means of reassurance to the believer. But should a sinner recognize that he lacked penitence where conscience proclaimed it due, it is time for him to fear for his salvation. Thus, for Calvin as for Luther, the part that penitence plays towards the assurance of forgiveness is secondary, while the part of faith is primary.

Such faith cannot be at second hand, but every elect person is, in his own right, in Christ by virtue of his faith. Every Christian is thus a king and priest before God. But God unites all the elect in his Holy Church. On earth the Church is the visible and organic means whereby the Christian lives in Christ; and the sacraments signify to him this union which he has with Christ. By the prophetic inspiration of the Holy Spirit, the Word is preached in the Church, to maintain Christians in the fellowship of his grace. But the visible Church is full of persons who are not being saved. The Word does not profit them, and the sacraments increase their guilt. For God suffers these tares amidst his wheat, in the fulfilment of his good purpose towards his elect. Thus the visible Church is, and ever was, only a symbol of that invisible and eternal Church known to God. It is, however, for the visible Church to bear witness to the holiness of God, which it does, according to Calvin, in two ways. First, when the congregation is assembled to divine worship, it begins by making a General Confession of sins. Each person does this for himself, though in union with the whole congregation. Thus the elect, by acknowledging their own unrighteousness, glorify God in his righteousness. And a second way in which the Church proclaims the holiness of God is by exacting from any Christian whose conduct gives scandal to the congregation, such penance as suffices to content the Church. From 1541, when Calvin's ministry was established in the free city-state of Geneva, until his death in 1564, Calvin's influence was such that the civil arm

I

compelled those sentenced by the ecclesiastical consistory to submit to public penance, which resembled *exomologesis* as described
by Tertullian. Thus, in Calvin's Geneva, this exemplary chastise-
ment, known in England as 'the French discipline', might fall
upon any citizen, and it certainly resulted in the moral reformation of social life. But the emphasis, in this discipline, was first
upon 'contenting the Church', in regard to the glory of God.
Reformation of life took second place. There was, of course, no
thought of penance being undertaken to obtain salvation, as in
Tertullian's day. The doctrine of penance taught by the Schoolmen Calvin rejected, not only for the absurdity of supposing
that man, the sinner, can offer *satisfactio* for his sins, but because
it so hedged the assurance of forgiveness with conditions as to
leave the scrupulous penitent always in doubt. 'Restless dubiety
of conscience', Calvin said, 'is among the primary axioms of our
opponents' doctrine'. In Calvin's eyes, this was a capital indict-
ment. If to be forgiven is to be elect, as Calvin taught, there is
nothing more indispensable than the assurance of forgiveness.
And this was what Calvin claimed to find and to minister in the
Reformed religion.

During the short reign of Edward VI in England, the established Church was feeling her way to the right use of her new
liberties. In general, she was moving with the cautious conservatism that seems to be a national characteristic. But her leaders
were wide awake to what was going forward on the continent.
In the early days of Edward's reign, a number of continental
Lutherans were received into offices in the ministry of the Church
of England. But Calvin was now at the height of his influence and
was in correspondence with the Protector Somerset and the
young King. The minds of several of those chiefly engaged in
equipping the English Church with a liturgy and formularies

were deeply impressed by the Church order of Geneva, if not wholly ready to embrace Calvin's doctrine. And Calvinism would, no doubt, have advanced, in England, had not the reign of Mary brought back the Roman obedience, and so broken up the tug-of-war between conservatism, Lutheranism and Calvinism that produced the Prayer Book of 1552. But when Elizabeth succeeded in 1558, it was this Book of Common Prayer which was authoritatively restored. The majority of Englishmen were glad to conform. As Elizabeth's reign proceeded, the political behaviour of Roman Catholicism towards the English Queen turned England decisively against it, but not towards Calvinism. There was indeed a very considerable body of English churchmen who embraced Calvinist principles. But these folk naturally adopted the Genevan severity of attitude towards dancing, gaming, the stage and other amusements. For this reason they were known as Puritans. The very nickname shows that they were out of touch with the social temper of the country. And keen as they were to establish the features of the Genevan theocracy in the life of the English Church, the attempt proved to be in vain.

On the other hand, Calvinism had already left a mark upon the Prayer Book, and in 1572 the Thirty-Nine Articles of Religion, put out by Convocation, had a markedly Calvinistic tint. As regards the forgiveness of sins, the most strikingly Calvinistic feature of the Prayer Book is the General Confession with which Morning and Evening Prayer begin. This is indeed a simple copying of Geneva. On the other hand, the exhortation, with which the Minister leads up to it, is not at all Calvinist in character. Formally, the so-called Absolution which follows is nothing but a preaching of the Gospel of forgiveness. But the rubric precludes it from being read except by a priest. Through this rubric, the committing of the 'power of the keys' to the priest at his ordination, extends to this reply to a general confession the associations of *absolvo te*, as people had been used to it in medieval penance.

Still less is the very contrite general confession made by the congregation about to receive communion suggestive of Calvinism, while the priest's answer, on that occasion, resembles an absolution much more than a mere preaching of the Gospel. If this were not enough to prove the deviation of Anglican thought, with regard to the forgiveness of sins, from the Calvinist standard, it would be more than made good from the Order for the Visitation of the Sick. It is here directed that a Christian who may be facing the approach of death shall be offered opportunity of receiving the assurance of forgiveness, by means of something that hardly differs from private penance as it was in use before the Reformation. Yet there is a difference, and it is a significant difference. For while the priest is authorized to pronounce an *absolvo te*, he is not authorized to name or demand a *satisfactio*. The discretion which he exercises is purely pastoral. He has, that is, to seek assurance that faith and repentance are present in the heart of the penitent, before he answers with the assurance of divine forgiveness. If he says, 'Will you take, for your penance ...?', he goes outside the doctrine of the Prayer Book; at least if the acceptance of the penance is regarded as anything more than a token of faith and repentance in the heart of the penitent. Thus it appears that, under the Elizabethan settlement of religion, Anglican churchmen were taught to seek the assurance of forgiveness by ways that were a following of neither Calvin nor the Schoolmen. And so the critical question is, whether the statements in the Prayer Book, on this, as on any other subject of doctrine, are coherent or not; in other words, whether the Anglicanism that rallied about this Book was doctrinally eclectic or syncretistic.

That this was a critical question, was evident to the Elizabethan churchmen. The classic answer was given, during that reign, by Richard Hooker, in his *Ecclesiastical Polity*.[1] It was to the effect that the Anglicanism of the Book of Common Prayer is eclectic. The truths which it asserts are maintained, some by one, and some by another, in systems mutually at war; but the truths cohere. The *Ecclesiastical Polity* is in eight books, of which Book VI treats of the forgiveness of sins. Unfortunately, this Book was not published in Hooker's lifetime. The draft which was published in 1648 may not be throughout authentically Hooker's work. It is, however, this draft that remains to be considered and it is unnecessary to speak of its teaching otherwise than as Hooker's. Hooker's general position, as against the Puritans, is that things not commanded in Scripture are not necessarily, therefore, against the law of God, which is expressed also through the principles of reason and natural order. Hooker accordingly set out to prove that Anglicanism, while emphatically scriptural, rests upon the more comprehensive law.

On the subject of the assurance of forgiveness, Hooker shows that the Church of England sides with the Reformed, against the Roman Catholics, in assigning to faith the first place. Repentance follows upon faith, being, as says the Augsburg Confession, no act of natural virtue. As Hooker now puts it, it arises only when God has opened the eye of the soul towards himself. There is a natural repentance, Hooker admits, which is based upon the thought of coming retribution. It has no kinship with Christian penitence. Even though the sinner may imagine that he is repenting in a Christian fashion, he will never, unless faith opens to him a vision of God, get beyond what might be defined as the attrition of the impenitent. For repentance is, as much as faith

[1] In *Works (with an account of his life and death by Isaac Walton)*, 1885, 2 vols.

itself, something that takes place within the heart. No external circumstance and no action on the part of other persons, can initiate faith or repentance, both being gifts of God. It is in vain, therefore, that the ministrations of the Church are expected to conjure repentance out of the remorse or fear that may have been roused in the heart of natural man. And this consideration disposes of the claim of penance to be a sacrament. Since Christian repentance is nothing natural, but is God-given, it can not, on the Scholastic definition of a sacrament, be the matter of a sacrament. So, by this refutation of the Scholastic doctrine of the forgiveness of sins, Hooker throws into relief the vital part played by inward penitence in the working out of our salvation.

Hooker took great comfort to himself from a work by an ancient writer, then recently made known to the Western public. The author was a pupil of Chrysostom, and lived in Asia Minor at the beginning of the fifth century. He is referred to as Mark the Hermit, and his work *Against the possibility of being justified by works* was printed in 1563 by Jean Picot, from a manuscript in the Royal Library at Paris.[1] Here, as Hooker saw, was a pre-Augustinian writer, wholly independent of that tradition of teaching on grace and free-will from which subsequent Western thought could not break free. Hooker cites, with satisfaction, the Marcan maxim, that 'No one was ever damned, except for despising repentance, or justified except for concerning himself to repent'.

What Hooker understood by 'concerning oneself to repent' may be judged from the teaching of Mark's master, Chrysostom, whose saying 'I exhort that men confess without ceasing' makes confession an act of private piety comparable with prayer. It is to be preceded by a strict and unsparing examination of conscience, and by the 'tears' that give evidence of repentance from

[1] In Migne *PG*, 65.903–1118.

the heart and of horror of relapse. The verbal confession which completes the act is as much a glorifying of God in his righteousness as it is self-accusation. Throughout the intervening centuries, the Eastern Church has continued to approach the subject in this manner, which, by comparison with the doctrine and practice of the West, might be characterized as unlegalistic.

Hooker goes on to observe that temptation is always baited with pleasure. Therefore, he argues, no aversion of the will from sin can take place without there being grief in the repenting. This grief is something which the Old Adam in us will not endure, so that he must be mortified. It is not natural to be willing to mortify the Old Adam in ourselves. So, when repentance has been born in the heart, there is still this obstacle to its completion. It is in this mortifying of the Old Adam that the Christian may be aided by the Church, moving him to a godly sorrow for his sins. The first way in which the Church of England seeks to give this aid to her people, Hooker sees to consist in the General Confession in the Prayer Book. This is not only, he says, the witness of the Church to the wrath of God against sin. It is to be used by each individual of the congregation, as an aid to godly sorrow for his own remembered sins. In like manner, each may take the Absolution as applying to himself, listening attentively to the declaration of the Gospel of forgiveness, thus renewing his faith, and embracing the assurance of forgiveness.

For the Church's next provision for the penitent, Hooker points to the private confession for which provision is made in the Order for the Visitation of the Sick. This was no freak of conservatism on the part of the drafters of the Order. There was a situation facing the Church of England, in the days of Queen Elizabeth I, which no doubt went far to commend it. It was the policy of the Queen and her bishops to oust the formerly prevalent non-communicating attendance at Mass in favour of parish communions, at which all the confirmed would communicate. In its execution, this policy encountered a formidable obstacle. This was the widespread superstitious dread of 'eating and drinking damnation'. What really underlay reluctance to communicate was, most often, impenitence. Therefore the Exhortations to Communion, provided in the Communion Service, plead for penitence and faith, in the hope of overcoming those natural obstacles which hinder response to grace.

An interesting question arising from the Book of Common Prayer, where there can be less assurance as to the background against which the drafting took place, is that raised by the Bishop's thanksgiving at the beginning of the Confirmation Service. He uses the words, 'who hast vouchsafed to regenerate these thy servants by Water and the Holy Ghost, and hast given unto them forgiveness of all their sins'. It is presumed that the candidates have come to years of discretion, and at least may have received baptism in their infancy. It would therefore be unreasonable to interpret 'all their sins' to the exclusion of actual sins. The model preparation for Confirmation is the Prayer Book catechism. This presupposes pastoral relations between the catechist and the young person under instruction, which has resulted in the candidate being conscious of having been called into a state of salvation and knowing it to be a blessing. There is set forth, in the 'duty towards God' and the 'duty towards my Neighbour', a pattern of life which, when understood, must prick the conscience. When therefore we find in the Communion Service that communicants are supposed to know how to examine their consciences, the knowledge may be presumed to have come to them in preparation for Confirmation. The pastoral duty of convicting of sin remained with the clergy, with the pulpit as the commonly acknowledged place for this ministry. But conscientious pastors can never have let the pulpit become a way of escape from more intimate and personal ministrations, least of all in the Christian training of adolescents. People need not therefore fall away from communion, knowing their way to the confessional, the vestry or the parson's study, as the case might be. So the superstitious fear of unworthy communicating is dismissed.

Another form of difficulty is also anticipated, in the Visitation Order, as well as in the Exhortations. This is what they term scruple or doubtfulness on the part of the penitent. Hooker treats this as arising from an unhappy relic of the old teaching, in the form of a notion that there must be a quantitative *satisfactio*. Misled by this notion, some who were ready to be truly penitent fell to doubting the sufficiency of their sorrow, in view of their sins, and so of the validity of their repentance. Hooker replies with the assurance that the godly sorrow of a penitent is not a measured satisfaction offered to God. With whatever intensity it is expressed, it is a mere token, whereby the penitent testifies his whole-hearted acceptance of the satisfaction made for him by Christ.

No penitent, therefore, need fear that the insufficiency of his acts of penitence will deprive him of forgiveness. It makes no difference whether his grief is in respect to a *crimen*, or to some sin of daily commission. In either case, he will be as sorry as his conscience can make him, and will leave the rest to the mercy of God. If we return, in the light of this consideration, to the penitent in view in the office for the Visitation of the Sick, it will be clear that Hooker did not understand the words 'if he feel his conscience troubled with any weighty matter' as though there were sins objectively more difficult for God to forgive than others. He took the words as referring to a fact of human psychology. The penitent's state of mind was irrationally troubled. This condition, adverse to the completion of a good repentance, might be dissipated by the administration of that 'power of the keys' that Christ entrusted to his Church. Of this ministry of reconciliation, Hooker says that it is a heavenly treasure carried in earthen vessels, but, while subject to the frustrations characteristic of all things human, it is efficacious in that for which it was ordained. We do not see, either in the Prayer Book or in Hooker's exposition, any acknowledgement of the distinction drawn by the Schoolmen, between mortal and venial sins. If we go by the standard of Article XIII, all deeds of the natural man devoid of faith have the nature of mortal sins, and all sins of believers might accordingly be said to be rendered, by their faith and penitence, venial. By Hooker's test, which is the emotion that accompanies sinning, sins called light differ from sins called weighty, only in that, involving less guilty pleasure, they call for less grief in repenting. That a man should be grievously troubled in his conscience over a weighty matter, Hooker would have held to be quite right. Nevertheless, the ministration of the Church to such a man aims not so much at the deepening of his sorrow as to help him find his way to full Christian faith in the all-sufficing work of Christ. To this end, the Church of England will have the priest speak with the authority of Christ and say 'I absolve thee'. This does not make the priest a judge. He speaks in answer to the grief of a believer over his sins. If he is deceived by an insincere confession, the solemn words of absolution that come from his lips beat the empty air. There is nothing real to which they can refer.

Hooker has another reason for disregarding the distinction between mortal and venial sins. This is that repentance is the same kind of interior act, which nothing external or circumstantial can initiate, whether the sins to be repented were slight or shocking. It belongs to the absolute character of Christian faith that the assurance of forgiveness should, in the end, be as great in the one case as in the other. We may observe that the division of sins into two categories has never, from the First Epistle General of St John onwards, led to definition of the graver category, whether called 'sins unto death', *crimina* or mortal sins. All these phrases are impressionist in character, and not definitive. The most laborious attempts (such as that of Père H. Rondet, S.J., *Théologie du Péché*, 1957) to give the value of definition to the words 'mortal' and 'venial' applied to sins can hardly be said to attain their end. Those who use the distinction of mortal and venial always advise the penitent to act as if what he thinks venial might be mortal. Whatever may be said for this as a practical method of dealing with repentance, it is not what is implied in the language of the Book of Common Prayer.

And we may observe, finally, that, by this principle of the inwardness of the birth of penitence, Hooker passes by altogether the once troublesome question of the repetition of post-baptismal repentance. The Gospel gives no ground for Christian faith to stumble at repeated penitence. If the need for further repentance ever gives cause for alarm, it is alarm lest impenitence should be masquerading as penitence. So often as present penitence is sincere, the fact that it has been preceded by repentances that were partial or insincere, does not empty it of efficacy. It follows that we do not need to think of two categories of repentance, one readily repeatable (in respect of venial sins) and another doubtfully repeatable (in respect of grave sins). We need only, with Calvin, establish the truth that the state of the elect is a state of continual penitence. It is not surprising if, as Cyprian found, repenting is the more sluggish the greater the guilt for

Epilogue

I T IS time for this story to draw to its conclusion, and for a brief summarizing of its tenor.

Forgiveness of sins is one aspect of that creative and redemptive act of God which, in its totality, is Christ. The understanding of it was not exhausted by the first generation of Christians. On the contrary, they could only see it with the partiality that was imposed upon them by their particular circumstances. Grand as was that phase of God's action in the Church whence the Scriptures of the New Testament were born, it was, nevertheless, a phase. We shall not expect, therefore, to find the whole understanding of our subject, for all time, explicit in the New Testament; though what is there written, when rightly expounded to the best of our ability and in dependence upon the guidance of the Spirit inspiring the Scriptures themselves, must be the test and canon of every subsequent development of doctrine. The New Testament begins an unfolding of our subject, which has been continued by means of Christian penitence and the apprehension of divine forgiveness in the experience of individuals. Belief in divine forgiveness of men's sins, through their faith in the satisfaction for all sin made by Christ, comes to us as the heart of a Gospel that is eschatological; which is to say, one in which divine incarnation figures, not as an incident in the world's history, but as something which indeed happened, but with once-for-all significance, so that, relative to ourselves, it is as much present as past. Accordingly the boon of baptism is not so much remission of sins to date, as entry, through faith in Christ, upon the forgiven life. This fact is testified by the painful struggle of early Christian thinkers to see how the forgiven life could continue, if the baptized sinned afresh, and still more in face of the repeated incidence of sins in the lives of the baptized.

When Augustine established the notion of timeless sin, as constituting part of the Christian tradition, the way began to be clear for a new appraisement of the continuance of sinning on the part of Christians. By that time, however, the fact of such sinning was inescapable. Also by that time the Western Church was engaged in a battle, that lasted throughout the Middle Ages, to gain and keep her hold over society in the young nations of Europe. In this task, she treated the sins of her members, and their regaining the assurance of forgiveness after their sinning, entirely in their character as incidents in the time-sequence. For the lay people, therefore, timeless sin had no practical meaning. They understood that the unbaptized would go to hell. But they were content in believing that Catholics, being baptized, had no more to fear from original sin. Meanwhile the Schoolmen built up a theology of sin and forgiveness, with sins as incidents countered by a corresponding reiteration of ecclesiastical penance.

To bring back an understanding of the forgiveness of sins as eschatological, in the primitive sense of the word, there was need of a revolution in Christian thought. Luther was the needed revolutionary. He saw that believing man stands before his Maker, timelessly, in himself a sinner and in Christ a saint. Now revolutions are always apt to go too far. The Lutheran and Reformed Churches reacted so heavily against the teaching and practice of penance accepted in Roman Catholicism as to overlook the fact that every man's spiritual life begins in a life of incident and of causal sequences; so that, if sin and forgiveness are denied a share in those conditions, Christianity is in danger of becoming mere otherworldliness. It is true that man is not so bound into the sequence of incidents that he cannot, in stillness, know the eternity of God. The fact that he can do so is, indeed, the most significant thing about him. But he is so far bound into that sequence that he can only know sin in terms of his own commission of sins. Now a believing Christian, though standing thus with a foot in each of two worlds, remains one indivisible person. And so, when he has, in solitude, been face to face with the ever holy God, in which experience he has known himself to be always and inescapably a sinner, he must presently turn back again to face, in active life, that human society that forms his little world. There it is a necessity of his nature that he should integrate for himself a personality that will command a measure of respect. And in as far as the society in which he lives is influenced by Christianity, he will try to do this by purging away vices and attaining to virtues. The Reformers were clearly right in denying that his degree of success in this endeavour makes any difference to his standing, as a forgiven sinner, before God. And yet the assimilation of the believer to Christ, proclaimed in Scripture to be the fulfilment of God's will, consists in just such a purging of vices and attaining to virtues. There is nothing amiss, therefore, with the fact and nature of the endeavour. The danger lies only in its motive; that is to say, in our shaping our conduct with our faces turned continually towards men. As long as a man, facing in that direction, thinks that he is, or intends to become, a very decent fellow, he cannot but find it ridiculous to proclaim himself a miserable sinner. But while he thinks in those terms, it goes without saying that his face is never truly towards God, as were the faces of the Reformers and of their principal teachers, Augustine and Paul. So then, for the understanding of the forgiven life, the first step is to learn to stand alone in the Presence of God, and to know oneself not worthy, but worse than worthless; to know oneself, in fact, the wanton and treacherous creature of an all-holy and perfect Creator. When a person returns from that moment in solitude to the life of incident in the society of men, and there falls again into particular sins, it will not take away from the universal truth of God's gratuitous love for man in Christ that he should make those sins the subject of particular repentances. In fact, it was not necessary that the Lutheran reaffirmation of the timeless relation of the soul with God should banish the use of the confessional, or any other legitimate means of reiterated faith and penitence on the part of a Christian sinner. There are, in fact, strong practical reasons for making such personal acts of penitence for particular sins. Until some such act is made, the Christian sinner is, and feels, 'tied and bound with the chain of his sins'. The clouded and unwilling memory of them is destructive of morale. They go on tainting his life at source. It is therefore of such great importance that there should be proclaimed, in the Gospel, not only that the Son of God has, in heaven, established for us a limitless opportunity of pardon, but further that (Mark 2.10) 'the Son of man hath power on earth to forgive sins'. Now the proclamation of 'power on earth to forgive sins' would have no virtue if it were not power to disengage the sinner from the earthly chains that he has made for himself by his sins. For once we have made them, we cannot unmake them by ourselves. But the believing sinner can hold up his chains to the Son of man who stands beside him, through his mystical Presence in his Church. For it is always in the actual and living Church that the written page of the Gospel comes alive. It is therefore possible for the Christian penitent to glorify God by a particular and present act of penitence, whatever legitimate form his penance takes, and as owing that possibilty to the Church. Thereafter, when, by faith, he knows himself once more to be innocent in God's sight, he finds also that the manacles have dropped from his hands. For the assurance of pardon restores moral liberty to the soul.

Also, unless people learn to recognize their own actual sins as a real cause for grief and repenting, and so come to want the assurance of God's forgiveness, they may never reach true Christian faith at all. If, on the other hand, they are not led beyond this stage but are left absorbing themselves in their own doings, all the labour of the Church to teach holiness and righteousness may do nothing but bring them to a self-righteousness which is the very opposite of a state of salvation. To reach their true goal, they must learn *metanoia* (conversion), the difficult facing-about, from looking to men to looking to God.

It is this complex of needs on the part of all Christian people that calls for the skill and wisdom of the Christian pastor. He has, on the one hand, to work for the rebirth of individuals into that life eternal which is God's free gift, and on the other hand to seek God's glory by promoting the holy and righteous living of the congregation entrusted to his care. It is a two-fold task, but indivisible. The second part can only be safely accomplished upon the basis of the first.

It seems, then, that the story that we have followed is more than the record of changing thought and tensions unresolved. It is rather the story of a building-up movement in Christianity towards a single integrated apprehension of divine forgiveness. We are the heirs of all that Christian past which we have been surveying. But we have each to enter for himself into living and active possession of this heritage. And herein is the need for trying to tell the story which forms the main content of this little book.

It remains to attempt a sketch of that belief in divine forgiveness to which this story may have led us. We stand first with Calvin, and following the pointer of the sacred history of man's fall, we contemplate ourselves in the Presence of God. So we see that we have in ourselves no active power except the power to sin. The gloom of the prospect that thus opens before us is such as could not be pierced by any ray of light unless and until it can be believed that God wills to save man in spite of himself.

We stand next with Luther, and viewing with horror the stream of actual sins that have, by our fault, flowed from that corrupted nature which we have inherited, come to appreciate the glorious meaning of the atonement wrought for us by Christ. Such a contemplation of actual sins is not, however, lightly accomplished, as in a flash of thought. Most Christians can only come to it by dealing, painfully, with the actual sins that burden their consciences at any particular time. And patterns for that dealing with actual sins have been brought before us in the story of catholic Christian thought upon this subject. In following that story through its successive stages, we learn to appreciate the gravity that sinning must have in the eyes of a Christian. We learn how proper it is that we should submit ourselves to suffer because of our sinning. We learn, further, how to use the repenting of less voluntary sins to the renewal of faith, and to the quest of sanctification. There is no disharmony between such a discipline and the insights of the Reformers.

The unity of such a doctrine and practice, with regard to the forgiveness of sins, is authentic unity, because the Reformers were not innovators, but revivers of the Gospel as testified by St

Paul. That Gospel was not 'another Gospel', different from the Gospel of the catholic Church, but is its fulfilment. And we therefore do nothing amiss in seeking a doctrine of forgiveness that is at once Catholic and Reformed.

Bibliography

More recent publications on Forgiveness of Sins

For New Testament teaching:
E. REDLICH, *The Forgiveness of Sins* (Edinburgh, 1937)
V. TAYLOR, *Forgiveness and Reconciliation* (London, 1941)

For the early patristic period:
O. WATKINS, *A History of Penance* (London, 1920)
R. S. T. HASLEHURST, *The Penitential Discipline of the Early Church in the first four centuries* (London, 1921)

For the doctrinal background for this period:
J. F. BETHUNE-BAKER, *Introduction to the Early History of Christian Doctrine*, Cc. 17, 18 (8th Edn, London, 1949)

J. N. D. KELLY, *Early Christian Doctrines* (London, 1958)

For the rise of private penance:
R. C. MORTIMER, *The Origins of Private Penance in the Western Church* (Oxford, 1939)

For the question of Attrition:
J. PÉRINELLE, *L'Attrition d'après le Concile de Trente* (Le Saulchoir, 1927)

For the Protestant doctrine of Christian perfection:
R. N. FLEW, *The Idea of Perfection in Christian Theology* (Oxford, 1934)

The rise of private penance is very fully treated by
B. POSCHMANN, *Die abendländische Kirchenbusse in Ausgang des christliche Altertums* (Breslau, 1928)
Die abendländische Kirchenbusse in früher Mittelalter (Breslau, 1930)

Paenitentia Secunda. Die kirchliche Busse im ältesten Christentum bis Cyprian und Origenes (Bonn, 1940)

See also C. VOGEL, *La discipline pénitentielle en Gaulle* (Paris, 1952)

The case for the antiquity of private penance is maintained by P. GALTIER, *L'Église et la remission des péches aux premiers siècles* (Paris, 1932), *Aux origines du sacrament de pénitence* (Rome, 1951) and by G. H. JOYCE in the *Journal of Theological Studies*, XLII, pp. 18–42.

Index

151